NEWCAS[
UNITED F.C.

- THE 25 YEAR RECORD

1970-71 to 1994-95 Seasons

SEASON BY SEASON WRITE-UPS
David Powter

EDITOR
Michael Robinson

CONTENTS

British Library Cataloguing in Publication Data
A catalogue record for this book is available from the British Library
ISBN 0-947808-54-X

Copyright © 1995; SOCCER BOOK PUBLISHING LTD. (01472-696226)
72, St. Peters' Avenue, Cleethorpes, Sth. Humberside, DN35 8HU, England

Printed by Redwood Books, Kennet House, Kennet Way, Trowbridge, Wilts.

NEWCASTLE UNITED
- Seasons 1970-71 to 1994-95

The 1994-95 campaign ended in disappointment for Newcastle United, who faded after an excellent start to finish 6th, and flattered to deceive in 3 cup competitions. The club's long run without winning a major trophy had continued - although prospects by the middle of 1995 looked better, than they had for many years.

The Magpies' most recent major trophy success was still fresh in fans' minds 25 seasons ago. They had won the European Fairs Cup in 1969 and 1970-71 was to be their third consecutive campaign in this competition. Their manager was Joe Harvey, who had masterminded both their European success and promotion back to the top-flight (4 terms earlier). Newcastle had finished in the top ten in each of the previous 3 seasons, gradually improving the final placing. However, a lack of goal power in 1970-71 caused them to slip back to 12th. Pop Robson's tally of 8 (out of a meagre total of 44) was still enough to make him the top scorer, even though he had moved to West Ham in the February.

The club's European campaign ended in the second round in Hungary. Harvey's side led by two Wyn Davies goals in the first leg, but Pecsi Dozsa levelled through a Bobby Moncur own-goal and a penalty on their own soil, before prospering in a penalty shoot-out.

In a bid to increase their goal-power Harvey replaced Davies with £180,000 signing Malcolm Macdonald before the start of the 1971-72 season. Supermac made an immediate impression, netting 23 of his team's 49 goals as they moved up one place to finish 11th.

Apart from Macdonald's fine start in the black and white stripes, Newcastle's 1971-72 campaign will always be remembered for their embarrassing exit from the FA Cup third round at the hands of the then Non-League Hereford United. After a 2-2 draw at St. James' Park, the Southern League outfit triumphed 2-1 at Edgar Street.

Despite a mixed start, United climbed into the top 5 at the end of 1972. However, they could not maintain their momentum and slipped back to 9th at the end of the season. The Magpies had scored more freely, with John Tudor the top scorer on 18, pipping Macdonald by one goal.

Newcastle successfully participated in the 1972-73 Anglo-Italian Cup. They won all 4 group games, beat Crystal Palace in a two legged semi-final and then won the trophy by defeating Fiorentina 2-1 in Florence.

The Magpies followed up with another trophy in 1973-74, but many of their fans saw the Texaco Cup as small beer in a season which at different times and in differing ways promised so much more.

After a mixed start, Newcastle roared into second place in November with 5 wins in six. With Macdonald absent injured, they suffered 4 straight defeats in December and after a brief revival on their centre-forward's return, only 2 wins were secured from the final 19 fixtures. A contributory factor was their distraction in 2 cup campaigns and their descent from the top to near the bottom of the table became quite a concern. Four consecutive draws in April ended their relegation worries; but even so they only finished 2 points above relegated Southampton, in 15th.

On the FA Cup front, the Magpies earned a home quarter-final tie with Second Division Nottingham Forest by knocking out 3 other lower Division outfits. The tie played on 9th March turned out to be one of the most dramatic and controversial in the club's history. Forest were awarded a penalty in the second half and home defender Pat Howard was dismissed for his vehement protests. The penalty was converted to give Forest a 3-1 lead. A section of the crowd then invaded the pitch, but after an 8 minute break, order was restored and the match continued. The ten men played out of the skins and triumphed 4-3!

That was not the end of the matter, however. Five days later a special F.A. Commission annulled the result of the game and ordered the match to be replayed on a neutral ground. That venue was Goodison Park; in fact it was needed twice as the first 120 minutes remained goalless. A single Macdonald goal finally divided the teams.

Nine days later the Magpies reached the FA Cup final for a then record eleventh time when two more Macdonald goals proved enough to beat Burnley at Hillsborough. However, Macdonald and his colleagues froze at Wembley and

Liverpool won the final 3-0 with Kevin Keegan netting twice.

Newcastle had already won the Texaco Cup by the time they reached Wembley. The club was one of 16 from England and Scotland which accepted invitations to participate in the tournament. After 7 games (including an abandonment) and two lots of extra-time, Newcastle met Burnley in the final at St. James' Park. Extra-time was, of course, necessary but Newcastle won 2-1 and Moncur lifted the trophy.

A few weeks later Bobby Moncur left St. James' Park and joined Sunderland. The former Scotland skipper made 296 League games for the Magpies and also performed courageously in many cup-ties, not least in the successful two-legged Fairs Cup final when he contributed 3 goals.

Moncur had gone, but much stayed the same in 1974-75. Newcastle defended the Texaco trophy and after 9 games (and extra-time in the final) eventually retained it. In the League, Macdonald scored 21 times to become the First Division's top scorer; and his side again finished a mediocre 15th.

Newcastle lost to lower opposition in both major cups in 1974-75 and so the St. James' Park faithful were a fairly discontented bunch in the summer of 1975. Consequently Joe Harvey bowed to public opinion and relinquished his position as manager after 13 seasons in the job. The former United skipper had turned an average Second Division side into trophy winners and a respected top-flight side. Harvey remained at the club almost up to his death (in 1989) in the backroom. The new manager was Gordon Lee, who arrived after a contractual tug-of-war with his previous employers Blackburn.

The Magpies lost all 4 of their games in the early season Anglo-Scottish tournament; but in contrast had two fine runs in the major Cup tournaments. They reached the final of the League Cup and the last eight of the FA Cup; however, they were defeated in both in the course of 8 days. A spectacular over-head effort by Dennis Tueart caused the Geordies' heart-ache at Wembley as Manchester City scored twice to one Alan Gowling goal; then their injury-hit side subsided 4-2 in the FA Cup at Derby.

Lee's side could not maintain any consistency in the 1975-76 League campaign and needed a last match victory over Spurs to claim their usual 15th berth. For the fourth time in 5 seasons, Malcolm Macdonald finished top-scorer (with 19 goals); however, controversially and to the disdain of the fans, Lee sold him to Arsenal (for £333,333) in the close-season. Lee could not handle big stars and Supermac was one of the biggest; so, despite the England striker's phenomenal Newcastle scoring record of 95 goals from 187 games, he was gone.

Six months later, so was Gordon Lee. With the Magpies on the heels of the leaders in 5th and 18 months of his contract left, Lee accepted an offer to manage Everton. He decided that it would be in the best interests of his family to work closer to where his children were being schooled (in Lancashire). He was also aware that the Geordie fans were never going to forgive him for selling Supermac.

The United players petitioned the Board to request that Lee's assistant Richard Dinnis be given the chance to manage the club. Initially Dinnis was appointed on a temporary basis, but after further unrest by some of the players, he was given the job of team manager to the end of the season. An 11 game unbeaten run took United onto the fringe of the 1976-77 title race, but they lost 4 of their last 5 games and had to settle for 5th. Nevertheless it was a fine achievement considering the mid-season unrest and also gave them a passport back to Europe.

With Dinnis at the helm, the Magpies opened up 1977-78 with a victory, but then lost 10 consecutive League games to lie bottom of the table. In addition, Second Division Millwall knocked them out of the League Cup at St. James' Park. However, some comfort was gained in the UEFA Cup, where Newcastle progressed to a second round clash with Bastia. Despite losing the away leg 2-1, United were favourites to reach the third round. However, it was the French side who enjoyed the game at St. James' Park, winning 5-2 on aggregate. The writing was on the wall for Dinnis and with exactly a third of the season gone, he was dismissed with Newcastle in 21st place on just 6 points.

Bill McGarry was appointed as the new manager and, after 3 straight wins in December, prospects looked a little brighter. However, they won only once more in 23 games and were relegated in 21st place. Only 7,600 turned up to watch the final home game, by which time the Magpies had been consigned to the Second Division after a gap of 13 seasons.

McGarry quickly rebuilt the team, spending a lot of money on the likes of Peter Withe, John Connolly, Colin Suggett, Mark McGhee and Jim Pearson. Terry Hibbitt was also signed for his second spell at the club. McGarry's side recovered from a poor start to reach the top five by Christmas, then disaster struck and they lost 7 out of eight and had to settle for a 1978-79 finish of 8th.

Results matched optimism for more than half of 1979-80, and with 16 fixtures left, McGarry's side led the table. However, they won just once more and lost all chance of promotion, finishing in 9th.

After a poor start to 1980-81, Bill McGarry was sacked and replaced by Chesterfield boss Arthur Cox, a surprise choice. Newcastle were woeful up front all term, netting just 30 goals. Nevertheless, they still managed to finish 11th. Former Tow Law forward Chris Waddle made his debut in the October.

Imrie Varadi's arrival gave the Magpies more goal power in 1981-82, but 6 defeats out of seven in the spring ended their promotion hopes. They finished 9th, Varadi top scoring with 18.

Cox pulled off a master-stroke during the summer of 1982, when he enticed Kevin Keegan to move to Tyneside from Southampton. Keegan scored on his debut at St. James' Park in front of over 36,000 and went on to finish as joint top scorer (with Varadi) with 21 goals. With Terry McDermott rejoining the club from Liverpool, hopes were high that good times were around the corner. However, it was not quite to be in 1982-83 as the Magpies found it difficult to hit a vein of consistency. When they did it was just too late to squeeze into the promotion frame, which they missed by 3 points in 5th.

The final piece in Cox's jigsaw was completed in the early part of 1983-84 when Peter Beardsley joined from Vancouver Whitecaps (for just £120,000). Keegan netted 27, Beardsley 20 and Waddle 18 as the Magpies rattled up 85 goals on their way to promotion. Only 2 of the last 16 games were lost, although Cox's side could not quite get on terms with the top two - Chelsea and Sheffield Wednesday - and finished 9 points adrift in third.

Keegan retired from playing after scoring in the last game against Brighton, in front of another 36,000 plus St. James' Park crowd. Much more of a shock was Arthur Cox's resignation 12 days later. Cox moved on to Derby (who had just

Paul Gascoigne pictured in his Newcastle days.

In his 92 League appearances appearances for the club, he scored 21 goals before his transfer to Tottenham for £2.3 million broke the British transfer record.

been relegated to Division Three), for apparently lower wages.

Jack Charlton moved into the manager's office in June 1984. Newcastle's return to the top-flight began with three victories. However, they quickly came down to earth, conceding 10 goals in 3 defeats before throwing away a 4-0 lead on QPR'S artificial pitch in a 5-5 draw. They slipped into the bottom half in November and remained there for the rest of 1984-85 without really being sucked into the relegation fight. Nevertheless they only finished 3 points above the thick black line in 14th place. During the latter part of the campaign 17 year-old Paul Gascoigne was introduced for 2 substitute appearances.

Charlton resigned at the start of 1985-86. He had been barracked by some of the fans in a friendly match with Sheffield United and also had a disagreement with his board. After 10 years as the club coach, former goalkeeper Willie McFaul stepped up to take the managerial reins. Newcastle were well placed in 4th after 10 games, but despite 5 straight wins in the new year, they gradually slipped to 11th.

The Magpies got off to a poor start in 1986-87, picking up only 2 points from the first 6 games. A 7 game unbeaten run in November and December pulled them off the bottom of the table; but they immediately slumped again, losing 8 of the next nine to drop back into trouble. However, with Beardsley and new signing Paul Goddard linking well together, survival was virtually secured with a 9 match unbeaten run. They finished 17th, 5 points clear of the drop.

After scoring 61 goals from 147 League games in his first spell on Tyneside, Peter Beardsley moved to Liverpool. His replacement was the Brazilian Mirandinha.

With Mirandinha, Goddard and Gascoigne scoring most of the goals, McFaul's side gradually moved into the top half after a mediocre start to 1987-88. They finished 8th with a late burst of scoring by Michael O'Neill making him the top scorer with 12.

Both £2 million Gascoigne (to Spurs) and Goddard (to Derby) had departed by the start of 1988-89 and, without them, United struggled, winning just one of their first seven. The board acted swiftly by sacking McFaul and attempting to lure back their former manager Arthur Cox. However, Cox resisted and remained at Derby, while United struggled on into December with results going from bad to worse and goals hard to come by.

Jim Smith joined as the new manager in early December. He immediately sold striker John Robertson back to Hearts after his failure to score (in 12 games) for Newcastle and bought Kevin Brock from his previous club QPR. Smith's arrival prompted 2 victories from 3 games, but the club's failure to win more than just another 3 times meant that they were relegated in 20th and bottom place. Mirandinha finished top scorer with 9 out of a meagre total of 32 goals.

The Brazilian departed shortly afterwards, but the signing of centre-forward

Mick Quinn (from Portsmouth) added more punch to the attack in 1989-90. He weighed in with 32 goals and the returning Mark McGhee added a further 19 as the Magpies rattled in 80 goals. However, Smith's side only won once in the last 4 games to finish third, 5 points off automatic promotion, in a play-off position.

Newcastle's promotion prospects still looked bright after their play-off semi-final first leg when they held Sunderland to a goalless draw at Roker Park. However, it was the Wearsiders who had the better of the return, winning 2-0.

After a promising start, United gradually drifted into the middle of the pack in 1990-91. Goals were again hard to come by and, despite a spell of just one defeat in 9 games, Jim Smith resigned near the end of March. His replacement was Ossie Ardiles. The Magpies' finished 11th, with a tally of just 49 goals.

Ardiles only lasted 11 months at the helm before he was sacked following a 5-2 defeat at Oxford in February 1992. His side were just one place off the bottom and had just leaked 15 goals in 4 games. Kevin Keegan was the surprise appointment to succeed the Argentinian. Despite a run of 5 defeats, Newcastle just survived relegation (by 4 points) in 20th place by winning their last 2 games. The 1991-92 top scorer was Gavin Peacock with 16.

With Sir John Hall finally gaining control of the club, serious money was now available for transfer dealing. Keegan recruited Barry Venison, John Beresford and Paul Bracewell during the close season. His side set off at lightning pace, clocking up 11 straight League wins. Robert Lee, Scott Sellars and finally Andy Cole (for £1.75 million) were all added to the squad and the Magpies finished 1992-93 as Endsleigh League Division One Champions with 96 points, a club record. David Kelly top scored with 24, while Cole added 12 from the same number of appearances.

Keegan sold Kelly to Wolves before the start of the 1993-94 campaign; but greatly strengthened his side when he enticed Peter Beardsley back to St. James' Park. After a mixed start, the Magpies gained momentum and by December had reached the top three of the Premiership. With Cole (34) and Beardsley (21) rattling in 55 goals between them, Newcastle maintained their form and won 10 out of the last 14 to secure third and qualify for the UEFA Cup. Cole finished as the Premiership's leading scorer.

The Magpies made a flying 29 point start from their first 11 games in 1994-95, but were gradually weighed down by injuries to key players. A disappointing UEFA Cup exit against Athletic Bilbao seemed to erode some of their confidence and then, early in 1995, the £7 million sale of Cole to Manchester United left them short of goal power.

After losing to Everton in the FA Cup quarter-final, Newcastle turned their attention to improving their League position; but they eventually had to settle for 6th place, and failed to qualify for another stab at the UEFA Cup. Nevertheless, Kevin Keegan entered the summer of 1995 determined to strengthen his squad and make a serious bid to give Newcastle United a first major trophy in almost 30 years.

Andy Cole in action against Chelsea before his record £7 million transfer.

St. James Park undergoing redevelopment before the 1995-96 Season

F.A. CUP COMPETITION

1970/71 SEASON
3rd Round
Jan 11 vs Ipswich Town (h) 1-1
Att: 32,150 Mitchell
Replay
Jan 13 vs Ipswich Town (a) 1-2
Att: 21,449 Robson

1971/72 SEASON
3rd Round
Jan 24 vs Hereford United (h) 2-2
Att: 39,381 Tudor, Macdonald
Replay
Feb 5 vs Hereford United (a) 1-2
Att: 14,313 Macdonald

1972/73 SEASON
3rd Round
Jan 13 vs Bournemouth (h) 2-0
Att: 33,930 Macdonald, Cave (og)
4th Round
Feb 3 vs Luton Town (h) 0-2
Att: 42,276

1973/74 SEASON
3rd Round
Jan 5 vs Hendon (h) 1-1
Att: 33,840 Howard
Replay (at Vicarage Road)
Jan 9 vs Hendon (a) 4-0
*Att: 15,385 Hibbitt, Tudor, Macdonald,
McDermott (pen)*
4th Round
Jan 26 vs Scunthorpe United (h) 1-1
Att: 38,913 McDermott
Replay
Jan 30 vs Scunthorpe United (a) 3-0
Att: 19,028 Macdonald 2, Barrowclough
5th Round
Feb 16 vs West Bromwich Albion (a) 3-0
*Att: 42,699 Tudor, Macdonald, Barrow-
clough*
6th Round
Mar 9 vs Nottingham Forest (h) 4-3
*Att: 54,500 Tudor, Moncur, McDermott
(pen), Craig D.J.
Match declared void and ordered to be
replayed*
Replay (at Goodison Park)
Mar 18 vs Nottingham Forest 0-0
Att: 40,685
2nd Replay (at Goodison Park)
Mar 21 vs Nottingham Forest 1-0
Att: 31,373 Macdonald
Semi-Final (at Hillsborough)
Mar 30 vs Burnley 2-0
Att: 55,000 Macdonald 2
FINAL (at Wembley)
May 4 vs Liverpool 0-3
Att: 100,000

1974/75 SEASON
3rd Round (at Maine Road by F.A. order)
Jan 3 vs Manchester City (a) 2-0
Att: 37,625 Nulty, Burns
4th Round
Jan 25 vs Walsall (a) 0-1
Att: 19,998

1975/76 SEASON
3rd Round
Jan 3 vs Queen's Park Rangers (h) 0-0
Att: 20,102

Replay
Jan 7 vs Queen's Park Rangers (h) 2-1
Att: 37,225 Craig T (pen), Gowling
4th Round
Jan 24 vs Coventry City (a) 1-1
Att: 32,004 Gowling
Replay
Jan 28 vs Coventry City (h) 5-0
*Att: 44,676 Gowling, Macdonald 2,
Cassidy, Burns*
5th Round
Feb 14 vs Bolton Wanderers (a) 3-3
Att: 46,880 Gowling, Macdonald 2
Replay
Feb 18 vs Bolton Wanderers (h) 0-0
Att: 52,760
2nd Replay (at Elland Road)
Feb 23 vs Bolton Wanderers 2-1
Att: 43,448 Gowling, Burns
6th Round
Mar 6 vs Derby County (a) 2-4
Att: 38,362 Gowling 2

1976/77 SEASON
3rd Round
Jan 8 vs Sheffield United (a) 0-0
Att: 30,513
Replay
Jan 24 vs Sheffield United (h) 3-1
Att: 36,375 Craig T, Burns, McCaffery
4th Round
Jan 29 vs Manchester City (h) 1-3
Att: 45,300 Gowling

1977/78 SEASON
3rd Round
Jan 7 vs Peterborough United (a) 1-1
Att: 17,621 Hudson
Replay
Jan 11 vs Peterborough United (h) 2-0
Att: 26,837 Craig T (pen), Blackhall
4th Round
Jan 28 vs Wrexham (h) 2-2
Att: 29,344 Bird, Blackhall
Replay
Feb 6 vs Wrexham (a) 1-4
Att: 18,676 Burns

1978/79 SEASON
3rd Round
Jan 16 vs Torquay United (h) 3-1
Att: 21,366 Robinson, Withe, Nattrass (pen)
4th Round
Jan 27 vs Wolverhampton Wands. (h) 1-1
Att: 29,561 Withe
Replay
Feb 22 vs Wolverhampton Wands. (a) 0-1
Att: 19,588

1979/80 SEASON
3rd Round
Jan 5 vs Chester (h) 0-2
Att: 24,548

1980/81 SEASON
3rd Round
Jan 3 vs Sheffield Wednesday (h) 2-1
Att: 22,458 Waddle 2
4th Round
Jan 24 vs Luton Town (h) 2-1
Att: 29,211 Clarke, Martin
5th Round
Feb 14 vs Exeter City (h) 1-1
Att: 36,984 Shoulder
Replay
Feb 18 vs Exeter City (a) 0-4
Att: 17,668

1981/82 SEASON
3rd Round
Jan 4 vs Colchester United (h) 1-1
Att: 16,977 Varadi
Replay
Jan 18 vs Colchester United (a) 4-3
*Att: 7,505 Waddle, Varadi, Saunders,
Brownlie*
4th Round
Jan 23 vs Grimsby Town (h) 1-2
Att: 25,632 Moore (og)

1982/83 SEASON
3rd Round
Jan 8 vs Brighton & Hove Albion (a) 1-1
Att: 17,711 McDermott
Replay
Jan 12 vs Brighton & Hove Albion (h) 0-1
Att: 32,687

1983/84 SEASON
3rd Round
Jan 6 vs Liverpool (a) 0-4
Att: 33,566

1984/85 SEASON
3rd Round
Jan 6 vs Nottingham Forest (a) 1-1
Att: 23,582 Megson
Replay
Jan 9 vs Nottingham Forest (h) 1-3 (aet.)
Att: 25,166 Waddle

1985/86 SEASON
3rd Round
Jan 4 vs Brighton & Hove Albion (h) 0-2
Att: 24,643

1986/87 SEASON
3rd Round
Jan 21 vs Northampton (h) 2-1
Att: 23,177 Goddard, Thomas A
4th Round
Jan 31 vs Preston North End (h) 2-0
Att: 30,495 Roeder, Goddard
5th Round
Feb 21 vs Tottenham Hotspur (h) 0-1
Att: 38,033

1987/88 SEASON
3rd Round
Jan 9 vs Crystal Palace (h) 1-0
Att: 20,203 Gascoigne
4th Round
Jan 30 vs Swindon Town (h) 5-0
*Att: 27,548 Jackson D, Gascoigne 2 (1 pen),
O'Neill, Goddard*
5th Round
Feb 20 vs Wimbledon (h) 1-3
Att: 28,796 McDonald

1988/89 SEASON
3rd Round
Jan 7 vs Watford (h) 0-0
Att: 24,086
Replay
Jan 10 vs Watford (a) 2-2 (aet.)
Att: 16,431 Brock, Mirandinha (pen)
2nd Replay
Jan 16 vs Watford (h) 0-0 (aet.)
Att: 28,370
3rd Replay
Jan 18 vs Watford (a) 0-1 (aet.)
Att: 15,115

1989/90 SEASON
3rd Round
Jan 6 vs Hull City (a) 1-0
Att: 10,743 O'Brien

13

4th Round
Jan 27 vs Reading (a) 3-3
Att: 11,989 Quinn, McGhee 2

Replay
Jan 31 vs Reading (h) 4-1
Att: 26,233 McGhee 2, Quinn, Robinson

5th Round
Feb 18 vs Manchester United (h) 2-3
Att: 31,748 McGhee (pen), Scott

1990/91 SEASON
3rd Round
Jan 5 vs Derby County (h) 2-0
Att: 19,748 Quinn, Stimson

4th Round
Feb 13 vs Nottingham Forest (h) 2-2
Att: 29,231 Quinn, McGhee

Replay
Feb 18 vs Nottingham Forest (a) 0-3
Att: 28,962

1991/92 SEASON
3rd Round
Jan 4 vs Bournemouth (a) 0-0
Att: 10,651

Replay
Jan 22 vs Bournemouth (h) 2-2 (aet.)
Att: 25,954 Hunt 2
Bournemouth won 4-3 on penalties

1992/93 SEASON
3rd Round
Jan 2 vs Port Vale (h) 4-0
Att: 29,873 Peacock 2, Lee, Sheedy

4th Round
Jan 23 vs Rotherham United (a) 1-1
Att: 13,405 Lee

Replay
Feb 3 vs Rotherham United (h) 2-0
Att: 29,005 Kelly, Clark

5th Round
Feb 13 vs Blackburn Rovers (a) 0-1
Att: 19,972

1993/94 SEASON
3rd Round
Jan 8 vs Coventry City (h) 2-0
Att: 35,444 Cole, Beardsley

4th Round
Jan 29 vs Luton Town (h) 1-1
Att: 32,216 Beardsley (pen)

Replay
Feb 9 vs Luton Town (a) 0-2
Att: 12,503

1994/95 SEASON
3rd Round
Jan 8 vs Blackburn Rovers (h) 1-1
Att: 31,721 Lee

Replay
Jan 18 vs Blackburn Rovers (a) 2-1
Att: 22,658 Hottiger, Clark

4th Round
Jan 28 vs Swansea City (h) 3-0
Att: 34,372 Kitson 3

5th Round
Feb 19 vs Manchester City (h) 3-1
Att: 33,219 Gillespie 2, Beresford

6th Round
Mar 12 vs Everton (a) 0-1
Att: 35,203

LEAGUE CUP COMPETITION

1970/71 SEASON
2nd Round
Sep 8 vs Bristol Rovers (a) 1-2
Att: 16,824 Dyson

1971/72 SEASON
2nd Round
Sep 8 vs Halifax Town (h) 2-1
Att: 19,930 Macdonald, Cassidy

3rd Round
Oct 6 vs Arsenal (a) 0-4
Att: 34,071

1972/73 SEASON
2nd Round
Sep 5 vs Port Vale (a) 3-1
Att: 10,370 Macdonald, Barrowclough, Craig

3rd Round
Oct 4 vs Blackpool (h) 0-3
Att: 19,810

1973/74 SEASON
2nd Round
Oct 8 vs Doncaster Rovers (h) 6-0
Att: 15,948 Robson 2, Macdonald 3, Clark

3rd Round
Oct 30 vs Birmingham City (a) 2-2
Att: 13,025 Gibb, McDermott

Replay
Nov 7 vs Birmingham City (h) 0-1
Att: 19,276

1974/75 SEASON
2nd Round
Sep 10 vs Nottingham Forest (a) 1-1
Att: 14,183 Macdonald

Replay
Sep 25 vs Nottingham Forest (h) 3-0
Att: 26,228 Macdonald, Burns, Keeley

3rd Round
Oct 8 vs Queen's Park Rangers (a) 4-0
Att: 15,815 Tudor, Macdonald 3

4th Round
Nov 13 vs Fulham (h) 3-0
Att: 23,774 Cannell, Macdonald, Cassidy

5th Round
Dec 4 vs Chester (h) 0-0
Att: 31,656

Replay
Dec 18 vs Chester (a) 0-1
Att: 19,000

1975/76 SEASON
2nd Round (Scheduled at Southport but played at Newcastle by agreement)
Sep 10 vs Southport (h) 6-0
Att: 23,352 Gowling 4, Cannell 2

3rd Round
Oct 7 vs Bristol Rovers (a) 1-1
Att: 17,141 Gowling

Replay
Oct 15 vs Bristol Rovers (h) 2-0
Att: 26,294 Craig T (pen), Nattrass

4th Round
Nov 11 vs Queen's Park Rangers (a) 3-1
Att: 21,162 Macdonald, Burns, Nulty

5th Round
Dec 3 vs Notts County (h) 1-0
Att: 31,114 McManus (og)

Semi-Final (1st leg)
Jan 14 vs Tottenham Hotspur (a) 0-1
Att: 40,215

Semi-Final (2nd leg)
Jan 21 vs Tott. Hotspur (h) 3-1 (agg. 3-2)
Att: 49,902 Gowling, Keeley, Nulty

FINAL (at Wembley)
Feb 28 vs Manchester City 1-2
Att: 100,000 Gowling

1976/77 SEASON
2nd Round
Sep 1 vs Gillingham (a) 2-1
Att: 11,203 Cassidy, Cannell

3rd Round
Sep 22 vs Stoke City (h) 3-0
Att: 27,143 Craig T (pen), Burns, Nattrass

4th Round
Oct 27 vs Manchester United (h) 2-7
Att: 45,300 Burns, Nattrass

1977/78 SEASON
2nd Round
Aug 31 vs Millwall (h) 0-1
Att: 21,861

1978/79 SEASON
2nd Round
Aug 29 vs Watford (a) 1-2
Att: 15,346 Pearson

1979/80 SEASON
2nd Round (1st leg)
Aug 29 vs Sunderland (a) 2-2
Att: 27,746 Davies, Cartwright

2nd Round (2nd leg)
Sep 5 vs Sunderland (h) 2-2 (aet.) (agg. 4-4)
Att: 30,533 Shoulder, Boam
Sunderland won 7-6 on penalties

1980/81 SEASON
2nd Round (1st leg)
Aug 27 vs Bury (h) 3-2
Att: 9,073 Rafferty 2, Shoulder

2nd Round (2nd leg)
Sep 2 vs Bury (a) 0-1 (aggregate 3-3)
Att: 4,348 Bury won on Away Goals

1981/82 SEASON
2nd Round (1st leg)
Oct 7 vs Fulham (h) 1-2
Att: 20,247 Barton

2nd Round (2nd leg)
Oct 28 vs Fulham (a) 0-2 (aggregate 1-4)
Att: 7,210

1982/83 SEASON
2nd Round (1st leg)
Oct 6 vs Leeds United (a) 1-0
Att: 24,012 Varadi

2nd Round (2nd leg)
Oct 27 vs Leeds United (h) 1-4 (agg. 2-4)
Att: 24,984 Clarke

1983/84 SEASON
2nd Round (1st leg)
Oct 5 vs Oxford United (h) 1-1
Att: 21,167 McDermott

2nd Round (2nd leg)
Oct 26 vs Oxford United (a) 1-2 (agg. 2-3)
Att: 13,040 Keegan

1984/85 SEASON
2nd Round (1st leg)
Sep 26 vs Bradford City (h) 3-1
Att: 18,121 McDonald, Ferris, Watson

2nd Round (2nd leg)
Oct 10 vs Bradford City (a) 1-0 (agg. 4-1)
Att: 10,210 Waddle

3rd Round
Oct 30 vs Ipswich Town (a) 1-1
Att: 15,084 McDonald

Replay
Nov 7 vs Ipswich Town (h) 1-2
Att: 22,982 Waddle

1985/86 SEASON
2nd Round (1st leg)
Sep 25 vs Barnsley (h) 0-0
Att: 18,544

2nd Round (2nd leg)
Oct 7 vs Barnsley (a) 1-1 (aet.)
Att: 10,084 Cunningham
Newcastle won on Away Goals

3rd Round
Oct 30 vs Oxford United (a) 1-3
Att: 8,096 Cunningham

1986/87 SEASON
2nd Round (1st leg)
Sep 23 vs Bradford City (a) 0-2
Att: 6,384

2nd Round (2nd leg)
Oct 8 vs Bradford City (h) 1-0 (agg. 1-2)
Att: 15,803 Roeder

1987/88 SEASON
2nd Round (1st leg)
Sep 23 vs Blackpool (a) 0-1
Att: 7,691

2nd Round (2nd leg)
Oct 7 vs Blackpool (h) 4-1 (aggregate 4-2)
*Att: 20,808 Goddard, Mirandinha, Jackson
D, Gascoigne*

3rd Round
Oct 28 vs Wimbledon (a) 1-2
Att: 6,443 McDonald (pen)

1988/89 SEASON
2nd Round (1st leg)
Sep 27 vs Sheffield United (a) 0-3
Att: 17,900

2nd Round (2nd leg)
Oct 12 vs Sheffield United (h) 2-0 (agg. 2-3)
Att: 14,520 Hendrie, Mirandinha

1989/90 SEASON
2nd Round (1st leg)
Sep 19 vs Reading (a) 1-3
Att: 7,960 Gallacher

2nd Round (2nd leg)
Oct 4 vs Reading (h) 4-0 (aggregate 5-3)
*Att: 15,220 Brazil (pen), Brock, Thorn,
McGhee*

3rd Round
Oct 25 vs West Bromwich Albion (h) 0-1
Att: 22,639

1990/91 SEASON
2nd Round (1st leg)
Sep 25 vs Middlesbrough (a) 0-2
Att: 15,042

2nd Round (2nd leg)
Oct 10 vs Middlesbrough (h) 1-0 (agg. 1-2)
Att: 12,778 Anderson

1991/92 SEASON
2nd Round (1st leg)
Sep 24 vs Crewe Alexandra (a) 4-3
Att: 4,251 Hunt, Peacock 3

2nd Round (2nd leg)
Oct 9 vs Crewe Alexandra (h) 1-0 (agg. 5-3)
Att: 9,197 Howey

3rd Round
Oct 29 vs Peterborough United (a) 0-1
Att: 10,382

1992/93 SEASON
1st Round (1st leg)
Aug 19 vs Mansfield Town (h) 2-1
Att: 14,083 Peacock 2

1st Round (2nd leg)
Aug 25 vs Mansfield Tn. (a) 0-0 (agg. 2-1)
Att: 6,725

2nd Round (1st leg)
Sep 23 vs Middlesbrough (h) 0-0
Att: 25,814

2nd Round (2nd leg)
Oct 7 vs Middlesbrough (a) 3-1 (agg. 3-1)
Att: 24,390 Kelly 2, O'Brien

3rd Round
Oct 28 vs Chelsea (a) 1-2
Att: 30,193 Lee

1993/94 SEASON
2nd Round (1st leg)
Sep 22 vs Notts County (h) 4-1
Att: 25,887 Cole 3, Bracewell

2nd Round (2nd leg)
Oct 5 vs Notts County (a) 7-1 (agg. 11-2)
*Att: 6,068 Allen 2 (1 pen), Beardsley, Cole
3, Lee*

3rd Round
Oct 27 vs Wimbledon (a) 1-2
Att: 11,531 Sellars

1994/95 SEASON
2nd Round (1st leg)
Sep 21 vs Barnsley (h) 2-1
Att: 27,208 Cole, Fox

2nd Round (2nd leg)
Oct 5 vs Barnsley (a) 1-0 (aggregate 3-1)
Att: 10,992 Cole

3rd Round
Oct 26 vs Manchester United (h) 2-0
Att: 34,178 Albert, Kitson

4th Round
Nov 30 vs Manchester City (a) 1-1
Att: 25,162 Jeffrey

Replay
Dec 21 vs Manchester City (h) 0-2
Att: 30,156

UEFA CUP
COMPETITION
1970/71 SEASON
1st Round (1st leg)
Sep 23 vs Inter Milan (a) 1-1
Att: 14,460 Davies

1st Round (2nd leg)
Sep 30 vs Inter Milan (h) 2-0 (agg. 3-1)
Att: 56,495 Davies, Moncur

2nd Round (1st leg)
Oct 21 vs Pecsi Dozsa (h) 2-0
Att: 50,550 Davies 2

2nd Round (2nd leg)
Nov 4 vs Pecsi Dozsa (a) 0-2 (aet) (agg 2-2)
Att: 25,000
Pecsi Dozsa won 3-0 on penalties

1977/78 SEASON
1st Round (1st leg)
Sep 14 vs Bohemians (a) 0-0
Att: 25,000

1st Round (2nd leg)
Sep 28 vs Bohemians (h) 4-0 (agg. 4-0)
Att: 19,046 Craig T 2, Gowling 2

2nd Round (1st leg)
Oct 19 vs Bastia (a) 1-2
Att: 8,500 Cannell

2nd Round (2nd leg)
Nov 2 vs Bastia (h) 1-3 (aggregate 2-5)
Att: 34,560 Gowling

1994/95 SEASON
1st Round (1st leg)
Sep 13 vs Antwerp (a) 5-0
Att: 19,700 Lee 3, Sellars, Watson

1st Round (2nd leg)
Sep 27 vs Antwerp (h) 5-2 (aggregate 10-2)
Att: 29,737 Lee, Cole 3, Beardsley (pen)

2nd Round (1st leg)
Oct 18 vs Athletic Bilbao (h) 3-2
Att: 32,140 Fox, Beardsley (pen), Cole

2nd Round (2nd leg)
Nov 1 vs Athletic Bilbao (a) 0-1 (agg. 3-3)
*Att: 47,000 Athletic Bilbao won on Away
Goals*

1970-71

1	Aug	15	(h)	Wolverhampton W	W	3-2	Foggon, Smith, Gibb		38,346
2		19	(a)	Stoke C	L	0-3			15,197
3		22	(a)	Crystal Palace	L	0-1			27,287
4		26	(h)	Nottingham F	D	1-1	McNamee		35,132
5		29	(h)	Blackpool	L	1-2	Hindson		34,041
6	Sep	2	(a)	West Brom A	W	2-1	Dyson, (og)		25,183
7		5	(a)	Derby Co	W	2-1	Young, Dyson		30,466
8		12	(h)	Liverpool	D	0-0			35,595
9		19	(a)	West Ham U	W	2-0	Robson 2		25,841
10		26	(h)	Coventry C	D	0-0			32,095
11	Oct	3	(a)	Manchester C	D	1-1	Ford		31,159
12		10	(h)	Arsenal	D	1-1	Robson		38,024
13		17	(a)	Wolverhampton W	L	2-3	Davies, (og)		24,083
14		24	(a)	Everton	L	1-3	(og)		43,135
15		31	(h)	Manchester U	W	1-0	Davies		45,176
16	Nov	7	(a)	Southampton	L	0-2			19,250
17		14	(h)	Ipswich T	D	0-0			25,657
18		21	(a)	Tottenham H	W	2-1	Gibb, Craig		38,873
19		28	(h)	Burnley	W	3-1	Ford, Robson, Moncur		20,994
20	Dec	5	(a)	Chelsea	L	0-1			39,413
21		12	(h)	Huddersfield T	W	2-0	Dyson, Robson		21,254
22		19	(h)	Crystal Palace	W	2-0	Robson 2 (1 pen)		21,779
23		26	(a)	Leeds U	L	0-3			46,758
24	Jan	9	(h)	Stoke C	L	0-2			25,708
25		16	(a)	Nottingham F	L	1-2	Robson		21,978
26		30	(a)	Burnley	D	1-1	Barrowclough		12,521
27	Feb	6	(h)	Chelsea	L	0-1			34,336
28		13	(a)	Huddersfield T	D	1-1	Smith		15,580
29		20	(h)	Tottenham H	W	1-0	Robson		31,718
30		27	(a)	Manchester U	L	0-1			41,902
31	Mar	13	(a)	Ipswich T	L	0-1			17,060
32		17	(h)	Everton	W	2-1	Tudor, Moncur		22,874
33		20	(h)	Southampton	D	2-2	Dyson 2		15,683
34		27	(h)	Derby Co	W	3-1	Dyson, Foggon 2		26,502
35	Apr	3	(a)	Blackpool	W	1-0	Foggon		14,637
36		6	(a)	Liverpool	D	1-1	Tudor		44,289
37		10	(h)	Leeds U	D	1-1	Tudor		49,699
38		12	(h)	Manchester C	D	0-0			29,148
39		17	(a)	Arsenal	L	0-1			48,106
40		24	(h)	West Ham U	D	1-1	Tudor		22,790
41		28	(h)	West Brom A	W	3-0	Young, Smith, Tudor		18,444
42	May	1	(a)	Coventry C	L	0-2			20,596

FINAL LEAGUE POSITION : 12th in Division One

Appearances

Sub. Appearances

Goals

McFaul	Craig	Guthrie	Gibb	McNamee	Moncur	Dyson	Robson	Davies	Smith	Foggon	Elliott	Ford	Hindson	Mitchell	Nattras	Arentoft	Barrowclough	Burleigh	Burton	Cassidy	Clark	Craggs	Tudor	Young	#
1	2	3	4	5	6	7	8	9	10	11															1
1	2	3	4	5	6	7	8	9	10	11															2
1	2	3	4	5	6	7	8	9		11						10									3
1	2	3	4	5	6	7	8	9	10			11													4
1	2	3	4	5	6	7*	8	9	10			11				12									5
1	2		4		6	8	7	9	10										5		3			11	6
1	2		4		6	8	7	9	10										5		3			11	7
1	2		4		6	8	7	9		11						10			5		3				8
1	2		4		6	8	7	9								10			5		3			11	9
1	2		4		6	8*	7	9				12				10			5		3			11	10
1	2		4		6	8	7	9				11				10			5		3				11
1	2		4		6	8	7	9				11				10			5		3				12
1	2		4		6	8	7	9				11				10			5*		3		12		13
1	2		4		6	8	7	9	10			11									3		5		14
1	2		4	5	6	8	7	9				11									3		10		15
1	2		4	5	6	12	7	9				11				10				8*	3				16
1	2		4	5	6		7	9	12	10		11								8*	3				17
1	2		4	5	6	8	7	9				11				10					3				18
1	2		4	5	6	8*	7	9				11		12		10					3				19
1	2		4	5	6	8	7	9				11				10					3				20
1	2		4	5	6	8	7*	9				11				10			12		3				21
1		3	4	5	6	8	7	9				11				10					2				22
	2		4	5	6	8	7	9				11						1			3		10		23
1	2		4	5	6	8	7	9						10							3		11		24
1	2		4	5	6	7	8	9		11						10					3				25
1	2	3	4		6		7	8	10								11		5			9			26
1	2	3	4		6		7	8	10								11		5			9			27
1	2	3	4		6		7	9	10										5			8		11	28
1	2	3	4		6		7	9	10										5			8		11	29
1	2	3	4		6			9	10				7						5			8		11	30
1	2	3	4		6			9	10										5	7		8		11	31
1	3*		4	5	6	7		9	10										12		2	8		11	32
1			4	5	6	9			10	7											3	2	8	11	33
1			4	5	6	9			10	7					12						3	2*	8	11	34
1			4	5	6				10*	7					12						3	2	8	11	35
1			4	5	6	9			10	7											3	2	8	11	36
1			4	5	6	9			10	7											3	2	8	11	37
1			4	5	6	9			10	7					12						3	2	8	11*	38
1			4	5	6	9			10	7											3	2	8	11	39
1			4	5	6	9			10	7											3	2	8	11	40
1			4	5	6	9		7	10												3	2	8	11	41
1	2		7	5		9		8	10						6						3	4		11	42
41	31	13	42	27	41	34	29	34	24	13	1	13	2	2	1	14	2	1	14	3	30	11	16	23	
						1				1		1		1	3	1			1	1				1	
	1		2	1	2	6	9	2	3	4		2	1			1							5	2	

1971-72

1	Aug	14	(a)	Crystal Palace	L	0-2		25,281
2		18	(a)	Tottenham H	D	0-0		42,715
3		21	(h)	Liverpool	W	3-2	Macdonald 3 (1 pen)	39,736
4		25	(h)	Huddersfield T	D	0-0		40,989
5		28	(a)	Coventry C	L	0-1		22,638
6	Sep	1	(a)	Leeds U	L	1-5	(og) (at Hillsborough)	18,623
7		4	(h)	West Ham U	D	2-2	Tudor, Cassidy	31,972
8		11	(a)	Manchester C	L	1-2	Macdonald	32,710
9		18	(h)	Wolverhampton W	W	2-0	Hibbitt, Tudor	29,347
10		25	(a)	Ipswich T	D	0-0		18,724
11	Oct	2	(h)	Derby Co	L	0-1		31,972
12		9	(a)	Arsenal	L	2-4	Macdonald 2	40,509
13		16	(h)	Crystal Palace	L	1-2	Dyson	20,711
14		23	(h)	Manchester U	L	0-1		55,603
15		30	(a)	Everton	L	0-1		38,811
16	Nov	6	(h)	Southampton	W	3-1	Macdonald 2, Green	32,677
17		13	(a)	Leicester C	L	0-3		28,792
18		20	(h)	Nottingham F	W	2-1	Macdonald 2	24,583
19		27	(a)	Stoke C	D	3-3	Macdonald 2, Craig D.J.	16,855
20	Dec	4	(h)	Chelsea	D	0-0		37,586
21		11	(a)	West Brom A	W	3-0	Busby, McDonald 2	18,036
22		18	(a)	West Ham U	W	1-0	Busby	21,991
23		27	(h)	Sheffield U	L	1-2	Hibbitt	53,079
24	Jan	1	(a)	Wolverhampton W	L	0-2		26,571
25		8	(h)	Coventry C	W	4-2	Hibbitt, Tudor 2, Macdonald (pen)	25,875
26		22	(h)	Tottenham H	W	3-1	Tudor, Macdonald, Nattrass	30,113
27		29	(a)	Huddersfield T	D	0-0		12,829
28	Feb	12	(a)	Manchester C	W	2-0	Tudor, Barrowclough	44,983
29		19	(h)	Everton	D	0-0		29,584
30		26	(a)	Southampton	W	2-1	Macdonald (pen), Barrowclough	18,884
31	Mar	4	(h)	Leicester C	W	2-0	Macdonald, Gibb	25,256
32		11	(h)	Arsenal	W	2-0	Macdonald, Smith	33,907
33		18	(a)	Liverpool	L	0-5		43,899
34		25	(h)	Manchester C	D	0-0		37,506
35	Apr	1	(a)	Sheffield U	L	0-1		28,103
36		3	(a)	Derby Co	W	1-0	Cassidy	38,119
37		5	(h)	Ipswich T	L	0-1		22,979
38		8	(a)	Nottingham F	L	0-1		12,470
39		19	(h)	Leeds U	W	1-0	Macdonald	42,164
40		22	(a)	Chelsea	D	3-3	Tudor 2, Macdonald	33,000
41	May	3	(h)	West Brom A	W	4-2	Macdonald 2 (1 pen), Green, (og)	18,927
42		8	(h)	Stoke C	D	0-0		21,264

FINAL LEAGUE POSITION : 11th in Division One

Appearances

Sub. Appearances

Goals

Player appearance & goals grid.

McFaul	Craig D.J.	Clark	Gibb	McNamee	Nattras	Dyson	Tudor	Macdonald	Young	Hibbitt	Cassidy	Hindson	Hodgson	Moncur	Howard	Barrowclough	Burleigh	Burton	Ellison	Green	Guthrie C	Guthrie R	Busby	Kennedy	Reid	Smith	
1	2	3	4	5	6	7*	8	9	10	11	12																1
1	2	3	4			7	8	9	10	11				6				5									2
1	2	3	4			7	8	9*	10	11	12			6				5									3
1	2	3	4			7	8	9	10	11				6				5									4
1	2	3	4				8	9	10	11	7			6				5									5
1	2	3	4	5			8	9		11	7			6								10					6
1	2	3	4				8	9		11	12	7		6*				5				10					7
1	2	6	4		10		8	9	12	11*	7							5				3					8
1	2	6	4		10		8	9		11				5	7							3					9
1	2	6	4		10		8	9		11				5	7							3					10
1	2	6	4		10		8	9		11				5	7				3								11
1		6			2	8	4	9	10	11	7			5					3								12
1		3	4			8	10	9	6	11	7			5					2								13
1		3	7		10		8*	9		11				6	12			5	2		4						14
1		3			12		10	9		11				6	7			5	2*	8	4						15
1	2	3	12		4		10	9		11*				6	7			5		8							16
1	2	3	12		4*		10	9		11				6	7			5		8							17
1	2	3			6		10	9		11				5	7					8			4				18
1	2	3			4		10	9		11				6	7*			5		8					12		19
1	2	3			4		10	9						6	11			5		8					7		20
1	2	3			4			9		11				6	12			5		8*		10			7		21
1		2	12		4			9		11				6	7*			5			3	8			10		22
1		2			4			9		11				6				5		8	3	10			7		23
1	2	3			4		10	9		11				6				5		8					7		24
	2	3			4*		10	9		11				6	7	1	5		8					12		25
1	2	3			4		10	9		11				6	7			5		8*					12		26
1	2	3	4		12		10	9		11				6	5	7*				8							27
1	2		4		12		10	9		11*				6	5	7				8							28
1	2	3	4				10	9		11				6	5	7				8	3						29
1	2	3	4				10	9		11				6	5	7				8							30
1	2	3	4				10	9		11*				6	5	7				8						12	31
1	2	3	4				10*	9		11				6	5	7				8						12	32
1	2	3	4				12	9		11				6	5	7				8						10*	33
1	2	3	4				10	9		11				6*	5	7				8					12		34
1	2	3	4				10	9						6	5	7				8					11		35
1	2	3	4*				10	9			12			6	5	7				8					11		36
1	2	3					10	9			11			6	5	7				8					4		37
1	2			4				9				11		6	5	7				8	10		3				38
1	2	3	4				10	9						6	5	7				8					11		39
1	2	3	4				10	9						6	5	7				8					11		40
1	2	3	4		12		10	9		11				6	5	7*				8					12		41
1	2	3	4		12		10	9		11				6	5					8					7*		42
41	36	40	26	2	20	6	37	42	7	35	5	2	1	21	34	26	1	19	5	27	3	8	4	1	12	1	
		3		4		1			1	4				2											6	2	
	1		1		1	1	8	23		3	2				2				2				2			1	

1972-73

1	Aug	12	(h)	Wolverhampton W	W	2-1	Tudor, Green	33,790
2		15	(a)	Birmingham C	L	2-3	Macdonald, Barrowclough	35,831
3		19	(a)	Sheffield U	W	2-1	Tudor, Macdonald	23,078
4		23	(h)	West Brom A	D	1-1	Macdonald	29,695
5		26	(h)	Ipswich T	L	1-2	Macdonald	24,601
6		30	(h)	Tottenham H	L	0-1		27,912
7	Sep	2	(a)	Crystal Palace	L	1-2	Tudor	21,749
8		9	(h)	Arsenal	W	2-1	Macdonald, Craig	23,878
9		16	(a)	Coventry C	W	3-0	Macdonald 3	17,592
10		23	(h)	Leeds U	W	3-2	Tudor, Macdonald, Smith	38,964
11		30	(a)	Everton	L	1-3	Barrowclough	33,028
12	Oct	7	(h)	Norwich C	W	3-1	Tudor 2, Guthrie	18,103
13		14	(a)	Stoke C	L	0-2		16,609
14		21	(h)	Manchester U	W	2-1	Hibbitt, Tudor	38,214
15		28	(a)	Chelsea	D	1-1	Smith	35,273
16	Nov	4	(a)	West Brom A	W	3-2	Tudor 2, Smith	14,379
17		11	(h)	Birmingham C	W	3-0	Macdonald, Howard, Gibb	26,042
18		18	(a)	Liverpool	L	2-3	Tudor, McDonald	46,153
19	Dec	2	(a)	West Ham U	D	1-1	Craig	23,785
20		9	(h)	Southampton	D	0-0		20,436
21		16	(a)	Derby Co	D	1-1	Tudor	28,826
22		23	(h)	Manchester C	W	2-1	Macdonald (pen), Barrowclough	28,274
23		26	(a)	Leeds U	L	0-1		45,486
24		30	(h)	Sheffield U	W	4-1	Macdonald, Tudor, Nattrass, Craig	28,620
25	Jan	1	(h)	Leicester C	D	2-2	Tudor, Smith	30,868
26		6	(a)	Ipswich T	L	0-1		19,609
27		20	(h)	Crystal Palace	W	2-0	Hibbitt, Nattrass	24,676
28		27	(a)	Arsenal	D	2-2	Macdonald, Smith	37,906
29	Feb	10	(h)	Coventry C	D	1-1	Barrowclough	23,051
30		17	(a)	Wolverhampton W	D	1-1	Hibbitt	22,147
31		24	(a)	Norwich C	W	1-0	Macdonald	26,411
32		28	(h)	Derby Co	W	2-0	Tudor, Macdonald	34,286
33	Mar	10	(h)	Stoke C	W	1-0	Macdonald	24,020
34		17	(a)	Manchester U	L	1-2	Nattrass	48,426
35		24	(h)	Chelsea	D	1-1	Barrowclough (pen)	24,663
36		31	(a)	Leicester C	D	0-0		18,712
37	Apr	7	(h)	West Ham U	L	1-2	Tudor	24,075
38		14	(a)	Southampton	D	1-1	Barrowclough	14,785
39		18	(a)	Manchester C	L	0-2		25,156
40		21	(h)	Liverpool	W	2-1	Tudor 2	36,810
41		25	(h)	Everton	D	0-0		22,390
42		28	(a)	Tottenham H	L	2-3	Tudor, McDermott	21,721

FINAL LEAGUE POSITION : 9th in Division One

Appearances

Sub. Appearances

Goals

McFaul	Craig	Clark	Gibb	Howard	Moncur	Barrowclough	Green	Macdonald	Tudor	Hibbitt	Hodgson	Kennedy	McDermott	Nattrass	Guthrie	Burleigh	Cassidy	Cowan	Reid	Robson	Smith	Young	
1	2	3	4	5	6	7	8	9	10	11													1
1	2	3	4	5	6	7	8	9	10	11													2
1	2	3	4	5		7*	8	9	10	11				12								6	3
1	2	3		5			8	9	10	11								4	7			6	4
1	2	3		5				9	10	11				12				4	8*	7		6	5
1	2	3		5		7	8	9	10	11				12				4*				6	6
1	2	3		5		7	8	9	10	11				4*				12				6	7
1	2	3		5	6	7		9	10	11											8	4	8
1	2	3		5	6	7		9	10	11											8	4	9
1	2	3	4	5		7		9*	10	11	12										8	6	10
1	2	3	4	5		7		9	11*	10	12										8	6	11
1	2		4	5	6	7		9	11	10			3								8		12
1	2	6	4	5		7		9	11	10			3								8		13
1	2	3	4	5	6	7		9	11	10											8		14
1	2	3	4	5	6	7		9	11	10*				12							8		15
1	2	5	4		6	7		9	10	11			3								8		16
1	2	3	4*	5	6	7		9	10	11				12							8		17
1	2	3		5	6	7		9	10	11				4							8		18
1	2	3		5	6	7		9	10	11				4							8		19
1	2	3		5	6	7		9	10	11				4							8		20
1	2	3		5	6	7		9	10	11				4							8		21
1	2	3		5	6	7		9	10	11				4							8		22
1	2	3		5	6	7		9	10	11				4							8		23
1	2	3		5	6	7		9	10	11				4							8		24
1	2	3		5	6	7		9	10	11				4							8		25
1	2	3		5	6	7		9	10	11				4							8		26
1	2	3		5	6			9	10	11				4	7						8		27
1	2	3		5	6	7		9	10	11				4							8		28
1	2	3		5	6	7		9	10					4					11		8		29
1	2	3		5	6	7		9	10	11				4					12		8*		30
1	2	3		5	6	7		9	10	11				4					8				31
	2	3		5	6	7		9	10	11				4		1					8		32
	2	6		5		7		9	10	11		3		4		1					8		33
	2	6		5		7		9	10	11		3	12	4		1					8*		34
	2	3		5	6	7		9		11			8	4		1				10			35
	2	3		5	6	7		9		11			8	4		1				10			36
	2	3		5	6	7		9	10	11				4		1					8		37
	2	3	4	5	6	7		9	10	11			8*	12		1							38
1	2	3	4*	5	6	7		9	10	11			8	12									39
1	2	3		5	6	7		9	10	11				4							8		40
1	2	3		5	6	7		9	10	11				4							8		41
1	2	3		5	6	7		9	10	11				4							8		42
35	42	41	13	41	32	39	6	35	42	41	5	2	7	21	3	7	1	3	3	2	32	9	
											1		1	4				2	2	2			
	3			1	1		6	1	17	18	3			1	3	1					5		

1973-74

1	Aug	25	(a)	West Ham U	W	2-1	Macdonald 2	28,169
2		29	(h)	Southampton	L	0-1		25,531
3	Sep	1	(h)	Arsenal	D	1-1	McDermott	30,665
4		4	(a)	Ipswich T	W	3-1	Robson, Cassidy, Smith	21,696
5		8	(a)	Sheffield U	D	1-1	Robson	26,897
6		12	(h)	Ipswich T	W	3-1	Macdonald 2, (og)	30,604
7		15	(h)	Wolverhampton W	W	2-0	Howard, Nattrass	36,412
8		22	(a)	Coventry C	D	2-2	Tudor, Macdonald	24,085
9		29	(h)	QPR	L	2-3	Tudor 2	31,402
10	Oct	6	(a)	Liverpool	L	1-2	Nattrass	45,612
11		13	(h)	Manchester C	W	1-0	Macdonald	35,346
12		20	(h)	Chelsea	W	2-0	Macdonald 2 (1 pen)	32,106
13		27	(a)	Tottenham H	W	2-0	Barrowclough, Gibb	31,259
14	Nov	3	(h)	Stoke C	W	2-1	Gibb, McDermott	28,135
15		10	(a)	Leicester C	L	0-1		20,726
16		17	(h)	Manchester U	W	3-2	Cassidy 2, Hope	42,474
17		24	(a)	Everton	D	1-1	Gibb	34,376
18	Dec	8	(a)	Birmingham C	L	0-1		25,428
19		15	(h)	Derby Co	L	0-2		19,470
20		22	(a)	QPR	L	2-3	Moncur, McDermott	15,757
21		26	(h)	Leeds U	L	0-1		55,638
22		29	(h)	Sheffield U	W	1-0	Tudor	27,943
23	Jan	1	(a)	Arsenal	W	1-0	Hibbitt	29,258
24		12	(a)	Wolverhampton W	L	0-1		22,235
25		19	(h)	West Ham U	D	1-1	Macdonald	27,217
26	Feb	2	(a)	Derby Co	L	0-1		24,992
27		5	(a)	Southampton	L	1-3	Macdonald	16,497
28		9	(h)	Coventry C	W	5-1	Tudor, Macdonald, Bruce, (2 ogs)	27,371
29		23	(h)	Liverpool	D	0-0		45,192
30	Mar	2	(a)	Leeds U	D	1-1	Barrowclough	46,611
31		16	(a)	Chelsea	L	0-1		24,207
32		23	(h)	Leicester C	D	1-1	McDermott (pen)	32,116
33		27	(a)	Manchester C	L	1-2	Cassidy	21,590
34	Apr	3	(a)	Stoke C	L	1-2	Tudor	16,437
35		6	(h)	Everton	W	2-1	Macdonald 2 (1 pen)	45,497
36		10	(h)	Burnley	L	1-2	Macdonald	30,168
37		13	(a)	Manchester U	L	0-1		44,751
38		15	(h)	Norwich C	D	0-0		31,132
39		17	(a)	Norwich C	D	1-1	Cassidy	18,408
40		20	(h)	Birmingham C	D	1-1	Robson	34,066
41		27	(a)	Burnley	D	1-1	Macdonald	21,340
42	May	11	(h)	Tottenham H	L	0-2		21,601

FINAL LEAGUE POSITION : 15th in Division One

Appearances

Sub. Appearances

Goals

Football appearances and goals grid (players across top, match number 1–42 at right):

McFaul	Craig D.J.	Clark	Gibb	Nattras	Moncur	Barrowclough	Smith	Macdonald	Tudor	Hibbitt	Bruce	Burleigh	Cannell	Cassidy	Hodgson	Hope	Howard	Hudson	Crosson	Kennedy	Laughton	McDermott	Robson	No.
1	2	3	4	5	6	7	8	9	10	11														1
1	2*	3	4	5	6	7	8			11						9	10			12				2
1		3		2	6	7	8			11				9			5			4		10		3
1		3		2	6	7	8			11				9			5			4		10		4
1		3		2	6	12	8*	9		11				7			5			4		10		5
1		3		2	6		8	9		11				7			5			4		10		6
1		3		2	6		8	9	10	11				7			5			4				7
1		3		2	6		8	9	10	11				7			5			4				8
1		3		2	6		8	9	10	11				7			5			4				9
1	12	3		2	6		8	9	10*	11				7			5			4				10
1	2	3		10*	6	12	8	9		11				7			5			4				11
1	2	3	12		6		8	9		11				7			5			4		10*		12
1	2	3	7		6	11	8	9	10								5			4				13
1	2	3	7		6	10	8			11				9			5	12		4*				14
1	2	3	7		6		8			11				10	9		5			4				15
1		3	7	2	6		8			11				10	9		5			4				16
1		3	7	2	6		8		10	11					9		5			4				17
1		3	12	2*		7	8	9		11							5			6	4	10		18
1		6		2		7		9		11				8			5		3		4	10		19
1	2	3	8		6			9		11				7			5			4		10		20
1	2	3	7		6	8*		9	10	11				12			5			4				21
1	2	3	7		6		8	9	10	11							5			4				22
1	2	6	7				8	9	10	11							5		3	4				23
1	2	6	7*			12		9	10	11				8			5		3	4				24
1	2	6				7	8	9	10				11				5		3	4				25
1	2	3	12		6	7	8	9	10*				11				5			4				26
1	2	3	4		6			9	10	11	7			8			5							27
1	2	3	4		6	12		9	10	11	7*			8			5							28
1	2	3			6	7*	11	9	10					8					12	4				29
1	2	5			6	7	11	9	10					8					3	4				30
1	2				6	7	8	9	10	11							5		3	4				31
1	2	5			6	7		9		11				8					3	4		10		32
	2	5			6			9		7		1	10	8		11			3		4			33
1	2	3			6			9		7				8		10	5			11	4			34
1	2	3			6			9	10	11	4			8		7	5							35
1	2*	3			6			9	10	11	4			8		7	5			12				36
1					6	7		9						8			5	2	3	11	4	10		37
1					6	7*		9	10	11	12			8			5	2	3		4			38
1					6			9	10					8			5	2	3	11	4		7	39
1					6			9	10					8			5	2	3	11	4		7	40
1	2				6	7		9	10					8			5		3	11	4			41
		12	7*					9	11	10		1		8			5	2	3	6	4			42
40	24	36	15	14	36	17	27	29	28	33	7	2	2	33	2	6	37	5	15	6	36	12		
	1		4		4					1			1							1		3		
		3	2	1	2	1	15	6	1	1				5			1	1				4	3	

1974-75

1	Aug	17	(h)	Coventry C	W	3-2	Macdonald, Howard, Kennedy	35,950
2		21	(h)	Sheffield U	D	2-2	Macdonald, Burns	34,283
3		24	(a)	Wolverhampton W	L	2-4	Tudor 2	23,526
4		27	(a)	Sheffield U	L	1-2	Keeley	17,650
5		31	(h)	West Ham U	W	2-0	Tudor, Macdonald	30,782
6	Sep	7	(a)	Derby Co	D	2-2	Macdonald, Burns	21,197
7		14	(h)	Carlisle U	W	1-0	Tudor	40,568
8		21	(a)	QPR	W	2-1	Tudor, Burns	18,594
9		28	(h)	Ipswich T	W	1-0	Howard	43,526
10	Oct	5	(a)	Everton	D	1-1	McDermott	40,000
11		12	(h)	Stoke C	D	2-2	Tudor, Keeley	39,658
12		16	(h)	Wolverhampton W	D	0-0		30,825
13		19	(a)	Birmingham C	L	0-3		33,339
14		26	(h)	Leicester C	L	0-1		34,988
15	Nov	2	(h)	Luton T	W	1-0	Tudor	30,141
16		9	(a)	Middlesbrough	D	0-0		39,000
17		16	(h)	Chelsea	W	5-0	Cannell, Macdonald 2, Kennedy, Barrowclough	35,236
18		23	(a)	Burnley	L	1-4	Barrowclough	19,523
19		30	(h)	Manchester C	W	2-1	Macdonald, Howard	37,684
20	Dec	7	(a)	Tottenham H	L	0-3		23,422
21		14	(a)	Coventry C	L	0-2		15,562
22		21	(h)	Leeds U	W	3-0	Tudor, Kennedy, Howard	34,054
23		26	(a)	Carlisle U	W	2-1	Tudor, Macdonald	20,605
24	Jan	11	(h)	Tottenham H	L	2-5	Craig T, Burns	39,679
25		18	(a)	Manchester C	L	1-5	Macdonald	32,021
26	Feb	1	(h)	Middlesbrough	W	2-1	Macdonald, Burns	42,514
27		8	(a)	Luton T	L	0-1		18,019
28		12	(h)	Liverpool	W	4-1	Tudor, Macdonald 2, Barrowclough	38,115
29		15	(h)	Burnley	W	3-0	Macdonald 2, Barrowclough	40,602
30		22	(a)	Chelsea	L	2-3	Tudor, Macdonald	26,770
31		28	(a)	West Ham U	W	1-0	Macdonald	33,150
32	Mar	15	(a)	Ipswich T	L	4-5	Tudor 2, Macdonald 2	23,450
33		18	(a)	Arsenal	L	0-3		16,540
34		22	(h)	Derby Co	L	0-2		32,201
35		25	(a)	Liverpool	L	0-4		41,147
36		29	(a)	Leeds U	D	1-1	Nulty	41,225
37		31	(h)	QPR	D	2-2	Tudor, Macdonald	29,819
38	Apr	5	(a)	Leicester C	L	0-4		23,132
39		12	(h)	Everton	L	0-1		29,585
40		19	(a)	Stoke C	D	0-0		32,302
41		23	(h)	Arsenal	W	3-1	Bruce, Macdonald, Craig T	21,895
42		26	(h)	Birmingham C	L	1-2	Macdonald	24,787

FINAL LEAGUE POSITION : 15th in Division One

Appearances

Sub. Appearances

Goals

24

McFaul	Nattrass	Kennedy	Smith	Keeley	Howard	Burns	Cassidy	Macdonald	Tudor	Hibbitt	Craig D	Barker	Barrowclough	Bell	Blackhall	Bruce	Clark	Craig T	Crosson	Gibb	Hudson	Kelly	Laughton	Cannell	Nulty	Mahoney	McCaffery	McDermott	
1	2	3*	4	5	6	7	8	9	10	11	12																		1
1	2	3	8	5	6	7		9	10	11																		4	2
1	2*	3	8	5	6	7		9	10	11	12																	4	3
1	8	3	5	6	7			9	10	11	2																	4	4
1	8		5	6	7			9	10	11	2					3												4	5
1	2		5	6	7	8		9	10	11						3				4									6
1	2	12	5	6	7	8		9	10	11						3				8								4*	7
1	2		5	6	7			9	10	11						3				8								4	8
1	2		5	6	7			9	10	11						3				8								4	9
1	2	3	5	6	7			9	10	11										8								4	10
1	2	3	5	6	7*			9	10	11			12							8								4	11
1	2	3	5	6	7			9	10	11										8								4	12
1	2	3	5	6	7			9	10	11										8								4	13
1		3	5	6	7		12	9	10	11						2				8								4*	14
1	2	8	5	6			4	9	10	11			7				3												15
1	2	8	5	6			4	9	10	11			7				3												16
1	2	8	12	5	6		4	9		11*			7				3							10					17
1	2	8	11	5	6		4	9*	12				7				3							10					18
1		8	11*	5	6		4	9			2		7			12	3							10					19
	2	8			6	7		9						1		11	3		4				5	10					20
1	2	8	5	6	7			9	10				12			11*	3			4									21
1	2	8	11	5				9	10				7				3			4									22
1	2	3	4	5	6			9	10				7					11							8				23
1	2	3	4	5	6	7		9	10									11							8				24
1	2	3	4	5	6	7		9	10*				12					11							8				25
1	2	3	4	5	6	10		9					7					11							8				26
1		3	4	5		10		9			2		7			6		11							8				27
1	2	3	4	5	6			9	10				7					11							8				28
1	2	3	4	5	6			9	10				7					11							8				29
1	2	3*	4	5	6	12		9	10				7					11							8				30
1	6		4	5				9	10		2	3	7					11							8				31
1	6*		4					9	10		2	3	7					11	12						8		5		32
1			4					9	10			3	7		6		2	11							8		5		33
1			4	5	6			9	10	3			7					11					2		8				34
1		4*		5	6			9	10	3	2		7				12	11							8				35
1	2			5	6			9	10	4	3		7					11							8				36
1	2			5	6			9	10*	4	3		7				12	11							8				37
1	2			5	6			9		3			7					11			4			10*	8	12			38
	2			5				9		11	3		7*			6	12		4					10	8	1			39
		3		5	12			9		11	2*		7			10	6	4							8	1			40
1		3		5	6	7*		9		11			7			10	2	4		12					8				41
1		3		5	6			9		11			7			10	2	4							8				42
39	33	28	19	39	36	21	8	42	31	25	13	2	23	1	1	5	19	19	1	11	1	1	1	7	20	2	2	12	
			2			1	1	1		1	2		3			3			1						2		1		
		3	2	4	5			21	14				4			1		2						1	1			1	

25

1975-76

								Att.
1	Aug	16	(a)	Ipswich T	W	3-0	Craig T (pen), Macdonald 2	27,680
2		20	(h)	Middlesbrough	D	1-1	Macdonald	41,417
3		23	(h)	Leicester C	W	3-0	Macdonald 2, Burns	36,084
4		27	(a)	Derby Co	L	2-3	Macdonald, Bruce	27,585
5		30	(a)	Manchester C	L	0-4		31,875
6	Sep	6	(h)	Aston Villa	W	3-0	Craig T, Macdonald 2	35,604
7		13	(a)	Everton	L	0-3		28,938
8		20	(h)	Wolverhampton W	W	5-1	Gowling 3, Tudor, Cassidy	30,876
9		23	(a)	Birmingham C	L	2-3	Craig T, Nulty	31,166
10		27	(a)	QPR	L	0-1		22,980
11	Oct	4	(h)	Tottenham H	D	2-2	Tudor, Barrowclough	33,284
12		11	(a)	West Ham U	L	1-2	Howard	30,400
13		18	(h)	Norwich C	W	5-2	Gowling 2, Macdonald 2, (og)	32,799
14		25	(a)	Stoke C	D	1-1	Gowling	24,057
15	Nov	1	(h)	Arsenal	W	2-0	Gowling, Nattrass	34,968
16		8	(a)	Leeds U	L	0-3		39,304
17		15	(h)	Liverpool	L	1-2	Nulty	41,145
18		22	(a)	Norwich C	W	2-1	Nulty 2	19,036
19		29	(a)	Manchester U	L	0-1		52,264
20	Dec	6	(h)	Coventry C	W	4-0	Craig T 2 (1 pen), Burns, Craig D	27,172
21		13	(a)	Leicester C	L	0-1		18,130
22		20	(h)	Ipswich T	D	1-1	Nulty	26,152
23		26	(a)	Burnley	W	1-0	Craig T (pen)	22,458
24		27	(h)	Sheffield U	D	1-1	Macdonald	31,762
25	Jan	10	(h)	Everton	W	5-0	Gowling 3, Nulty, Nattrass	31,726
26		17	(a)	Aston Villa	D	1-1	Gowling	36,389
27		31	(a)	Middlesbrough	D	3-3	Gowling, Kennedy, Nattrass	31,000
28	Feb	7	(h)	Derby Co	W	4-3	Craig T (pen), Macdonald, Nulty, (og)	45,770
29		21	(a)	Liverpool	L	0-2		43,404
30	Mar	3	(h)	Stoke C	L	0-1		38,822
31		13	(h)	West Ham U	W	2-1	Craig T (pen), Macdonald	33,866
32		16	(a)	Arsenal	D	0-0		18,424
33		20	(h)	Manchester U	L	3-4	Gowling, Macdonald, Burns	45,043
34		27	(a)	Coventry C	D	1-1	Bird	14,144
35		31	(h)	Leeds U	L	2-3	Craig T (pen), Gowling	32,685
36	Apr	3	(h)	QPR	L	1-2	Gowling	30,145
37		7	(h)	Birmingham C	W	4-0	Gowling, Macdonald 2, Burns	18,893
38		10	(a)	Wolverhampton W	L	0-5		20,083
39		14	(h)	Manchester C	W	2-1	Macdonald, Cassidy	21,095
40		17	(h)	Burnley	L	0-1		24,897
41		19	(a)	Sheffield U	L	0-1		18,906
42		24	(a)	Tottenham H	W	3-0	Macdonald 2, Burns	29,649

FINAL LEAGUE POSITION : 15th in Division One

Appearances

Sub. Appearances

Goals

Mahoney	Nattrass	Kennedy	Nulty	Howard	Hibbitt	Burns	Bruce	Macdonald	Gowling	Craig T	Barrowclough	Bird	Blackwell	Cannell	Cassidy	Craig D	Hudson	Jones	Keeley	MacLean	McCaffery	Oates	Tudor	
1	2	3	4	5	6	7	8	9	10	11														1
1	2	3	4	5	6	7	8*	9	10	11	12													2
1	2	3	4	5	6	7	8	9	10	11														3
1	2	3	4	5	6	7	8*	9	10	11	12													4
1	2	3	4	6		7		9	10	11		8			5									5
1	2	3	4	6		7		9	10	11		5			8									6
1	2	3	4	6		7			10	11	12	5			8							9*		7
1	2	3	4	6		7			10	11		5			8							9		8
1	2	3	4	6		7			10	11		5			8							9		9
1	2	3	11	6		7		9	10			5							4			8		10
1	2	3	4	6		7		9	10	11	12	5										8*		11
1	2	3	4	6		7		9	10	11		8			5									12
1	2	3	4	6		7		9	10	11		8			5									13
1	2	3	4	6		7*		9	10	11		8	12		5									14
1	2	3	4	6		7		9	10	11		8			5									15
1	2	3	4	6		7		9	10	11		8			5									16
1	2	3	4	6		7		9	10	11		8			5									17
1	2	3	4	6		7		9	10	11		8			5									18
1	2	3	4	6		7*		9	10	11		8			5								12	19
1	2	3	4	6		7		9	10	11		8			5									20
1	2	3	4	6		7		9	10	11		8			5									21
1	2	3	4	6		7		9	10	11		8			5									22
1	2	3	4	6		12		9	10	11					7	5						8*		23
1	2	3	4	6				9	10	11		8			7	5								24
1	2	3	4	6		8		9	10	11		5			7									25
1	2	3	4	6		7		9	10*	11	12	5			8									26
1	2	3	4	6		7		9	10	11					8				5					27
1	2	3	4	6		7		9	10	11							8		5					28
1	2	3		6		7		9	10	11		4			8	5*			12					29
1		3		6		7		9*		11		4	2	10	8	12			5					30
		3		6		7		9	10	11		4	5		2	8		1						31
		3		6		7		9	10	11		4	5		2	8		1						32
	2	3		6		7		9	10	11		4	5		8*			1				12		33
1	2	3	6*			7		9	10	11		4	5			12						8		34
1	2	3				7		9	10	11		4	5		8							6		35
1	2	3				7		9	10	11		4	5		8							6		36
1	2	3				7		9	10			4	5		11	8						6		37
1	2	3				7		9	10	12		4*	5		11	8						6		38
1	2	3				7		9	10	11		5*			4	8					12	6		39
1	2	3				7		9	10	11			12		4	8					5	6		40
	2	3				7		9	10	11					4	8		1		12	5	6*		41
	2	3				7		9	10	11					4		1	8			5	6		42
37	39	42	28	34	4	40	4	39	41	39	23	19	3	1	20	14	7	5	4	1	3	9	6	
										1	5		1			2			1	1	1	1	1	
	3	1	7	1		5	1	19	16	9	1	1			2	1							2	

27

1976-77

1	Aug	21	(h)	Derby Co	D	2-2	Craig T (pen), Hudson	35,927
2		25	(a)	Tottenham H	W	2-0	Burns, Barrowclough	24,022
3		28	(h)	Bristol C	D	0-0		31,775
4	Sep	4	(a)	Middlesbrough	L	0-1		26,000
5		11	(h)	Manchester U	D	2-2	Burns, Cannell	39,037
6		18	(a)	Leeds U	D	2-2	Cannell, Cassidy	35,098
7		25	(h)	Liverpool	W	1-0	Cannell	34,813
8	Oct	2	(a)	Norwich C	L	2-3	Craig T (pen), Gowling	21,417
9		6	(h)	West Brom A	W	2-0	Gowling, Cannell	28,746
10		16	(a)	Coventry C	D	1-1	Gowling	18,083
11		23	(h)	Birmingham C	W	3-2	Craig T, Burns 2	31,711
12		30	(h)	Stoke C	W	1-0	Cannell	32,339
13	Nov	6	(a)	Manchester C	D	0-0		40,049
14		20	(a)	West Ham U	W	2-1	Burns, Nulty	21,324
15		24	(h)	Everton	W	4-1	Craig T, Gowling 2, Cannell	31,203
16		27	(h)	QPR	W	2-0	Burns, Cannell	39,045
17	Dec	4	(a)	Arsenal	L	3-5	Gowling, Burns 2	35,000
18		18	(a)	Aston Villa	L	1-2	Gowling	33,982
19		27	(h)	Sunderland	W	2-0	Cannell, Kennedy	49,644
20	Jan	22	(a)	Derby Co	L	2-4	Craig T (pen), Gowling	23,036
21	Feb	5	(a)	Bristol C	D	1-1	Burns	28,000
22		16	(h)	Manchester C	D	2-2	Burns 2	28,954
23		19	(a)	Manchester U	L	1-3	Nulty	51,828
24		26	(h)	Tottenham H	W	2-0	Gowling, Burns	30,230
25	Mar	2	(h)	Leeds U	W	3-0	Burns, Oates, McCaffery	33,714
26		5	(a)	Liverpool	L	0-1		45,553
27		9	(h)	Ipswich T	D	1-1	Nattrass	33,820
28		12	(h)	Norwich C	W	5-1	Craig T, Gowling, Oates, McCaffery 2	27,808
29		15	(a)	Stoke C	D	0-0		12,708
30		19	(a)	West Brom A	D	1-1	Barrowclough	23,780
31		23	(h)	Coventry C	W	1-0	Burns	25,332
32		26	(h)	Middlesbrough	W	1-0	Kennedy	33,643
33	Apr	2	(a)	Birmingham C	W	2-1	Craig T (pen), Barrowclough	20,283
34		8	(a)	Sunderland	D	2-2	Craig T, Cannell	50,048
35		9	(h)	Leicester C	D	0-0		32,300
36		16	(h)	West Ham U	W	3-0	Gowling, Cannell Nulty	30,967
37		23	(a)	QPR	W	2-1	Barrowclough, Nattrass	20,544
38		30	(h)	Arsenal	L	0-2		44,677
39	May	3	(a)	Leicester C	L	0-1		14,289
40		7	(a)	Ipswich T	L	0-2		24,760
41		14	(h)	Aston Villa	W	3-2	Cannell 2, Oates	29,873
42		24	(a)	Everton	L	0-2		25,208

FINAL LEAGUE POSITION : 5th in Division One

Appearances

Sub. Appearances

Goals

Mahoney	Nattrass	Kennedy	Hudson	Bird	Nulty	Barrowclough	Oates	Burns	Gowling	Craig T	Cannell	Cassidy	Craig D	Blackhall	Guy	Howard	McCaffrey	Mitchell	Tudor	
1	2	3	4	5	6	7	8	9	10	11										1
1	2	3	4	5	6	7	8	9*	10	11				12						2
1	2	3	4	5	6	7	8			11*	9					12		10		3
1	2	3	4		6	7		9	10	11*	12	8				5				4
1	2	3			6	7		9	10	11	8	4				5				5
1	2	3			6	7	10	9		11	8	4				5				6
1	2	3			6	7	10	9		11	8		4*	12		5				7
1	2	3			6	7		9	10	11	8	4				5				8
1	2*	3			6	7	12	9	10	11	8	4				5				9
1	2	3			6	7		9	10	11	8	4				5				10
1	2	3*			6	7		9	10	11	8	4		12		5				11
1	2	3			6	7		9		11	8	4			10	5				12
1	2	3			6	7		9	10	11	8	4				5				13
1	2	3			6	7		9	10	11	8	4				5				14
1	2	3*			6	7		9	10	11	8	4	12			5				15
1	2	3			6	7		9	10	11	8	4				5				16
1	2	3			6	7		9	10	11	8	4				5				17
1	2	3			6	7		9	10	11	8	4				5				18
1	2	3			6	7		9	10	11	8	4				5				19
1	2	3			6	7		9	10	11	8	4				5				20
1	2	3			6	7	12	9	10	8*		4		11		5				21
1	2	3			6	7		9	10			4		11		5	8			22
1	2	3			6	7		9	10	11		4				5	8			23
1	2	3			6	7*	12	9	10	11		4				5	8			24
1	2	3			6	7	8	9	10	11		4				5				25
1	2	3			6	7	8	9	10	11		4*		12		5				26
1	2	3			6	7	8	9	10	11			4			5				27
1	2	3			6	7	8	9	10	11			4			5				28
1	2	3			6	7	8	9	10	11		4				5				29
1	2	3			6	7		9	10*	11		4		12	8	5				30
1	2	3			6	7		9	10*	11	8	4		12		5				31
1	2	3			6	7		9	10	11	8	4				5				32
1	2	3			6	7		9	10	11	8	4				5				33
1	2	3			6	7		9	10	11	8	4				5				34
1	2	3			6	7		9	10	11		4		8		5				35
1	2	3			6	7		9	10	11	8	4*		12		5				36
1	2	3			6	7		9	10*	11	8	4		12		5				37
1	2	3			6	7		9	10	11	8	4*		12		5				38
1	2*	3	12		6	7		9		11	8	4		10		5				39
1		3			6	7	10	9		11	8	4		2		5				40
1	2*	3			6		7	9	10	11	8	4		12		5				41
1		3		5	6	4	7	9	10	11	8									42
42	40	42	4	4	42	41	13	41	36	40	29	35	2	7	2	38	3	1		
			1				3						1	10	1					
	2	2	1		3	4	3	14	11	8	12	1					3			

1977-78

1	Aug	20	(h)	Leeds U	W	3-2	Burns 2, Kennedy	36,700
2		23	(a)	Liverpool	L	0-2		48,267
3		27	(a)	Middlesbrough	L	0-2		26,712
4	Sep	3	(h)	West Ham U	L	2-3	Burns, Cassidy	26,942
5		10	(h)	West Brom A	L	0-3		22,705
6		17	(a)	Birmingham C	L	0-3		18,953
7		24	(h)	Coventry C	L	1-2	Gowling	22,484
8	Oct	1	(a)	Ipswich T	L	1-2	McCaffery	21,797
9		5	(a)	Norwich C	L	1-2	Craig T	16,630
10		8	(h)	Derby Co	L	1-2	Burns	26,578
11		15	(a)	Manchester U	L	2-3	Martin, Burns	55,056
12		22	(h)	Chelsea	W	1-0	Burns	23,683
13		29	(a)	Everton	D	4-4	Craig T, Gowling 2, Cassidy	37,574
14	Nov	5	(h)	Bristol C	D	1-1	Martin	23,321
15		12	(a)	Wolverhampton W	L	0-1		16,964
16		19	(h)	Arsenal	L	1-2	Cassidy	23,679
17	Dec	3	(h)	Leicester C	W	2-0	Burns, Nattrass	20,112
18		10	(a)	QPR	W	1-0	Robinson	15,251
19		17	(h)	Wolverhampton W	W	4-0	Craig T, Mitchell, Cassidy, Nattrass	22,982
20		26	(a)	Manchester C	L	0-4		45,811
21		28	(h)	Nottingham F	L	0-2		41,612
22		31	(h)	Liverpool	L	0-2		36,499
23	Jan	2	(a)	Leeds U	W	2-0	Burns 2	36,643
24		14	(h)	Middlesbrough	L	2-4	McGhee, Cassidy	34,460
25		21	(a)	West Ham U	L	0-1		25,461
26	Feb	25	(h)	Ipswich T	L	0-1		22,264
27	Mar	4	(a)	Derby Co	D	1-1	Burns	19,708
28		11	(h)	Manchester U	D	2-2	McGhee, Burns (pen)	25,825
29		15	(h)	Birmingham C	D	1-1	Nattrass	19,493
30		18	(a)	Chelsea	D	2-2	McGhee, Burns (pen)	22,777
31		24	(h)	Everton	L	0-2		28,933
32		25	(a)	Nottingham F	L	0-2		35,552
33		29	(h)	Manchester C	D	2-2	Bird, Kennedy	20,256
34	Apr	1	(a)	Bristol C	L	1-3	Barrowclough	17,344
35		4	(a)	Coventry C	D	0-0		22,135
36		8	(h)	Aston Villa	D	1-1	Burns (pen)	19,330
37		12	(a)	West Brom A	L	0-2		17,053
38		15	(a)	Arsenal	L	1-2	Burns	33,353
39		19	(a)	Aston Villa	L	0-2		25,495
40		22	(h)	QPR	L	0-3		13,463
41		26	(h)	Norwich C	D	2-2	Burns, Kennedy	7,986
42		29	(a)	Leicester C	L	0-3		11,530

FINAL LEAGUE POSITION : 21st in Division One

Appearances

Sub. Appearances

Goals

Mahoney	Nattrass	Kennedy	Cassidy	McCaffery	Bird	Barrowclough	Cannell	Burns	Gowling	Craig T	Hardwick	Blackwell	Oates	MacLean	Mitchell	Craig D	Callachan	Blackley	Kelly	Martin	Nulty	Barker	Walker	Smith	Robinson	Carr	Hudson	Gorry	Larnach	
1	2	3	4	5	6	7	8	9	10	11																				1
	2	3	4	5	6	7	8*	9	10	11	1	12																		2
	2*	3	4	5	6	7		9	10	11	1	12	8																	3
1	12	3	4	5	6			9		11		2		10	7	8*														4
1	6	3		5	7	8		9	10*	11		4		12			2													5
1	6	3		5	7	8		9		11				12	4*		2	10												6
1	6	3	5		7			9	10	11				12	4*		2	8												7
1	6	3	5		7			9	10	11				12	8	2*	4													8
1	6	3	5		7			9	10	11		2		12	4		8*													9
1	2			5	7			9	10*	11		3	8	4				6	12											10
			5	4*	7	8		9		11	1	3		12				6	2	10										11
		3	4	5	7	8		9	10	11	1	2						6												12
		3	4	5	7			9	10	11	1	3	8					6												13
	2			5	7			9	10	11	1	6	8									3	4							14
	6		4	5	7			9		11	1				2			8				3	10*				12			15
	6		4	5	7			9	10*	11	1				2			12				3	8							16
	2		4	5			8		10		1			9				6	7			3	11							17
	2		4	5			8*	9	10									6	7			3	11	1	12					18
	2		4	5			8	9	10									6	7			3	11	1						19
	2		4	5			8	9	10									6*	7			3	11	1				12		20
	2		4	5	12	9*	8		10			6							7			3	11	1						21
	2			5	7*		8		10			6						12				3	11	1	4			9		22
			4	5	12		8		11			2										3				1	7	9		23
	6		4	5			8	10	11			2										3*	12			1	7			24
1	2	6	4*	5	11		7	12														3					8		10	25
1	2	10	4	5	7		8	11				6										3						9		26
1	4	3		5	7		8					6		2								12	11					9		27
1	4	3		5	7*		8					6		2									11					9		28
1	4	3		5			8					6		2								11*			7			9		29
1	2	3		5			8					6*		12								11						9		30
1	2	3		5	12		8*											6				11						9		31
1	2	3		5	7									9				6			8	11								32
1	2	3		5	7		8							9				6				11								33
1	2	3		5*	7		8							6								9	11							34
1	5	3			7		8					2					10	6												35
1	5	3			7		8					2					10*	6											12	36
1	5	3		12	7		8					2		6			10													37
1	5	3			7		8					2									6		10							38
1	5	3			7		8	9				2									6		10							39
1	2	3			7		8	9				5									6		11*						10	40
		3			7		8					5				6		2					11			1			10	41
							8						3			6	11	2		5		12				1			10	42
24	37	26	17	14	25	30	9	41	14	24	9	14	4	6	8	6	9	18	7	9	11	14	14	1	7	9	4	13		
	1			1	3				1			2	5	1					2	2		1				1	1	1	1	
		3	3	5	1	1	1	15	3	3				1						2					1					

1978-79

1	Aug	19	(a)	Millwall	L	1-2	Barton		12,105
2		23	(h)	West Ham U	L	0-3			27,167
3		26	(h)	Luton T	W	1-0	Pearson		24,112
4	Sep	2	(a)	Cambridge U	D	0-0			8,174
5		9	(h)	Blackburn R	W	3-1	Withe 2, McGhee		23,751
6		16	(a)	Wrexham	D	0-0			14,091
7		23	(h)	Orient	D	0-0			26,361
8		30	(a)	Notts Co	W	2-1	Connolly, Bird		11,362
9	Oct	7	(h)	Leicester C	W	1-0	Walker		25,731
10		14	(a)	Sunderland	D	1-1	Withe		35,405
11		21	(a)	Charlton Ath	L	1-4	Walker		11,616
12		28	(h)	Cardiff C	W	3-0	Connolly, Withe, Robinson		23,477
13	Nov	4	(a)	Bristol R	L	0-2			10,582
14		11	(h)	Millwall	W	1-0	Pearson		23,087
15		18	(a)	Luton T	L	0-2			10,434
16		22	(h)	Cambridge U	W	1-0	Bird		20,004
17		25	(h)	Oldham Ath	D	1-1	McGhee		20,563
18	Dec	2	(a)	Crystal Palace	L	0-1			19,761
19		9	(h)	Stoke C	W	2-0	Connolly, White		23,459
20		16	(a)	Fulham	W	3-1	Connolly, Withe, Shoulder		8,575
21		23	(h)	Burnley	W	3-1	Withe, Shoulder, Cassidy		23,639
22		26	(a)	Sheffield U	L	0-1			23,200
23		30	(a)	Brighton & HA	L	0-2			25,812
24	Feb	3	(a)	Orient	L	0-2			7,251
25		17	(a)	Leicester C	L	1-2	Nattrass		15,106
26		24	(h)	Sunderland	L	1-4	Connolly		34,733
27	Mar	3	(h)	Charlton Ath	W	5-3	Connolly, Shoulder 2 (1 pen), Martin, Mitchell		14,998
28		10	(a)	Cardiff C	L	1-2	Connolly		11,368
29		24	(a)	West Ham U	L	0-5			24,651
30		31	(a)	Oldham Ath	W	3-1	Withe, Shoulder (pen), Nattrass		6,329
31	Apr	4	(h)	Preston NE	W	4-3	Connolly, Withe, Shoulder, Barton		12,167
32		7	(h)	Crystal Palace	W	1-0	Shoulder		18,862
33		10	(a)	Burnley	L	0-1			7,851
34		14	(h)	Sheffield U	L	1-3	Shoulder		19,126
35		16	(a)	Preston NE	D	0-0			12,960
36		18	(h)	Notts Co	L	1-2	Withe		12,017
37		21	(h)	Fulham	D	0-0			11,924
38		25	(a)	Blackburn R	W	3-1	Withe 3		4,902
39		28	(a)	Stoke C	D	0-0			23,217
40	May	2	(h)	Bristol R	W	3-0	Withe, Shoulder, Bird		9,627
41		5	(h)	Brighton & HA	L	1-3	Shoulder		28,434
42		8	(h)	Wrexham	W	2-0	Peason, Shoulder		7,134

FINAL LEAGUE POSITION : 5th in Division Two

Appearances

Sub. Appearances

Goals

Mahoney	Kelly	Barker	Cassidy	Bird	Barton	Walker	Pearson	Mitchell	Hibbitt	Connolly	Blackley	Brownlie	Carr	Guy	Hardwick	Manners	Martin	McGhee	Mulgrove	Nattrass	Nicholson	Parkinson	Robinson	Scott	Shoulder	Suggett	Wharton	Withe	
1	2	3	4	5	6	7	8	9	10	11																			1
1	2	3	4	5		7	9		10	11	6															8			2
1	2	3	4	5			8		10	11	6															7		9	3
	2		4	5	6		8		10	11		3			1											7		9	4
	2	4*		5			8		10	11	6	3			1			12								7		9	5
	2	4		5				12	10	11	6	3			1			8*								7		9	6
	2	4						12	10	11	6*	3			1			8	5							7		9	7
	2		5					12	10	11	6	3			1			8*					4			7		9	8
	2*		5			8	4		10	11	6	3			1			12								7		9	9
	2		5	6	8	4			10	11		3			1											7		9	10
	2		5	6	8	7*	4		10			3			1					11						12		9	11
	2		5		8				10	11	6	3			1			12				4*				7		9	12
	2		5				8	4	10	11	6	3			1											7		9	13
	2		5				8	4*	10	11	6	3			1			12								7		9	14
	2*			5			8	4	10	11	6	3			1			12								7		9	15
		3	5				8		10		6	2			1			12	4	11						7*		9	16
		3	5				8	12	10		6	2			1		7		4*	11								9	17
			5		8*	3			10	11	6	2			1		4		12							7		9	18
		7	5			3			10	11	6	2			1		4							8				9	19
		8	5	12		3			10	11	6*	2			1		4							7				9	20
	12	8	5			3			10	11	6*	2			1		4							7				9	21
		8		5		3			10	11	6	2			1		4							7				9	22
		8		5		3			10	11		2			1		4			12				7	6*			9	23
				5		3			10		6	2	12		1		4	8				11*		7				9	24
				5		12	3				6	2			1		4	8				11*	10	7				9	25
			5		8		12		10	11	6*	2			1		4	3						7				9	26
			5		8	3			10	11		2			1		4*	6		12				7				9	27
			5		8	3			10	11		2			1		4	6						7*		12		9	28
			5		8*	3			10	11		2			1		4	6						7			12	9	29
		8	5						10	11	3	2			1		4	6						7				9	30
		8		5		6			10	11	3	2			1		4							7				9	31
		8		5					10	11	3	2			1		4	6						7				9	32
		8		5					10	11	3	2			1		4	6						7				9	33
		8					5		10	11	3	2			1		4	6						7				9	34
		8				12	5		10	11	3	2	1				4*	6						7				9	35
		8				4		5	10	11*	3	2	1					6						7		12		9	36
			3	5	10		9				2*	1					4	6		11				7	8		12	9	37
			6	5				3	10				1				4	2		11				7	8			9	38
			6	5				3	10				1				4	2		11				7	8			9	39
			6	5				3*	10	11			1	4				2		12				7	8			9	40
			6	5				3*	10	11			1	4	8			2		12				7				9	41
			6	5		8		3	10	11			1	4				2						7				9	42
3	15	5	19	27	21	18	9	26	40	34	28	34	8		31	2	23	4	21	5		4	2	24	20			39	
	1			1	2	5								1				6	1			3	1			3	2		
		1	3	2	2	3	1		8							1	2		2			1		11				14	

33

1979-80

#	Month	Date		Opponent	Result		Scorers	Attendance
1	Aug	18	(h)	Oldham Ath	W	3-2	Withe, Shoulder 2 (2 pens)	19,099
2		21	(a)	Preston NE	L	0-1		12,707
3		25	(a)	Charlton Ath	D	1-1	Cassidy	6,849
4	Sep	1	(h)	Chelsea	W	2-1	Withe 2	25,047
5		8	(a)	Orient	W	4-1	Cartwright, Hibbitt, Withe, Shoulder (pen)	5,700
6		15	(h)	Leicester C	W	3-2	Cartwright, Shoulder 2 (2 pens)	26,443
7		22	(h)	Wrexham	W	1-0	Shoulder (pen)	27,904
8		29	(a)	Birmingham C	D	0-0		19,967
9	Oct	6	(a)	West Ham U	D	1-1	Withe	23,206
10		10	(h)	Preston NE	D	0-0		25,154
11		13	(h)	Shrewsbury T	W	1-0	Shoulder	21,603
12		20	(a)	Watford	L	0-2		17,715
13		27	(h)	Cambridge U	W	2-0	Withe, Shoulder	24,104
14	Nov	3	(a)	Oldham Ath	L	0-1		11,486
15		10	(h)	Cardiff C	W	1-0	Shoulder	22,867
16		17	(a)	Bristol R	D	1-1	Shoulder	7,626
17		24	(a)	Swansea C	W	3-2	Hibbitt, Rafferty, Shoulder	15,442
18	Dec	1	(h)	Fulham	W	2-0	Rafferty, Withe	23,485
19		8	(a)	Luton T	D	1-1	Rafferty	14,845
20		15	(h)	QPR	W	4-2	Withe 2, Shoulder, Cassidy	25,027
21		22	(a)	Notts Co	D	2-2	Shoulder, Connolly	11,224
22		26	(a)	Burnley	L	2-3	Shoulder, Barton	16,433
23		29	(h)	Charlton Ath	W	2-0	Shoulder, Cassidy	26,225
24	Jan	1	(h)	Sunderland	W	3-1	Cartwright, Shoulder (pen), Cassidy	38,784
25		12	(a)	Chelsea	L	0-4		32,281
26		19	(h)	Orient	W	2-0	Connolly, Barton	20,954
27	Feb	2	(a)	Leicester C	L	0-1		24,549
28		9	(a)	Wrexham	L	0-1		13,299
29		20	(h)	Birmingham C	D	0-0		27,069
30		23	(a)	Shrewsbury T	L	1-3	Shoulder (pen)	10,833
31	Mar	1	(h)	Watford	L	0-2		23,091
32		8	(a)	Cambridge U	D	0-0		6,908
33		15	(h)	West Ham U	D	0-0		25,474
34		22	(a)	Cardiff C	D	1-1	Shinton	9,304
35		29	(h)	Bristol R	W	3-1	Withe 2, Cassidy	18,975
36	Apr	2	(h)	Notts Co	D	2-2	Shoulder, Cassidy	22,005
37		5	(a)	Sunderland	L	0-1		41,752
38		7	(h)	Burnley	D	1-1	Davies	18,863
39		12	(a)	Fulham	L	0-1		7,152
40		19	(h)	Swansea C	L	1-3	Shoulder (pen)	14,314
41		26	(a)	QPR	L	1-2	Ferguson	11,245
42	May	3	(h)	Luton T	D	2-2	Shoulder, Rafferty	13,765

FINAL LEAGUE POSITION : 9th in Division Two

Appearances

Sub. Appearances

Goals

34

Hardwick	Brownlie	Davies	Martin	Barton	Bird	Shoulder	Cassidy	Withe	Hibbitt	Pearson	Boam	Carney	Carr	Cartwright	Connolly	Cropley	Ferguson	Mitchell	Nicholson	Rafferty	Shinton	Walker	Wharton	
1	2	3	4	5	6	7	8	9	10	11														1
1	2	3	4	5	6	7	8	9	10	11														2
1	2	3	4	5	6	7	8	9	10					12					11*					3
1	2	3	4	5		7	8*	9	10		6			11				12						4
1	2	3	4	5		7	8*	9	10		6			11								12		5
1	2	3	4	5		7	8	9	10		6			11										6
1	2	3	4	5		7	8	9	10		6			11										7
1	2	3	4	5		7	8	9	10		6			11										8
1	2	3	4	5		7		9	10		6			11								8		9
1	2	3	4	5		7		9	10		6			11								8		10
1	2		4	5		7	8	9	10		6					3				11				11
1	2	3	4	5		7	8*	9	10		6			12	11									12
1	2	3	4	5		7	12	9*			6			11						10	8			13
1	2	12	4	5		7		9			6			11		3				10	8*			14
1	2	3	4	5		7		9	11		6									10	8			15
1	2	3	4	5		7		9	11*		6			8	12					10				16
1	2	3	4	5		7		9	11		6			8*	12					10				17
1			4	5		7		9	11		6	2		8			3			10				18
1	2	4*	5			7		9	11		6	3		8	12					10				19
1	2	3	5			7	4	9	11		6			8*	12					10				20
1	2	3	5			7	4	9*	11		6			8	12					10				21
1	2	3	5			7	4*		11		6	12		8	9					10				22
1	2	3	5			7	4		11		6			8	9					10				23
1	2	3	5			7	4	9	11		6			8						10				24
1	2	3	5			7	4	9	11		6			8	12					10*				25
1	2	3	5			7	4	9			6	10		8	11									26
1	2	3*	5			7	4	9			6	10		8	11					12				27
1	2	3	5			7*	4	9			6	5		8	11	10				12				28
1		3				7	4	9			5	2		8	11	10*		6		12				29
1	2					7		9	11		5	3		8	12	4*		6		10				30
1	2	3*	5			7	4	9	11		6			8	10					12				31
1	2	3			6		4	9	10		5			8							11	7		32
1	2	3			6	4			10		5			8						9	11	7		33
1	2	3			6	4		9	10		5			8							11	7		34
1	2	3			6	12	4	9			5			8							11	7*		35
1	2	3			6	7	4	9			5			8							11			36
1		3			6	7	4	9	10		5	2		8*							11	12		37
1		3			6	7	4	9*			5	2					12			10	11	8		38
1	2	3			6	11	4		10		5			8						9	7			39
1	2		5			11	4*		10		6			12		8				9	7	3		40
1	2	3				11*	4	9			5			8		10	6				12	7		41
	2	3			6	11		9	10		5		1	4	8						7			42
41	38	36	19	32	9	40	29	37	34	2	38	10	1	33	8	3	4	6	1	19	10	11	1	
		1				1	1				1			3	7	1			1	5		2		
		1		2		20	6	11	2					3	2		1			4	1			

1980-81

								Attendance
1	Aug	16	(a)	Sheffield W	L	0-2		26,164
2		20	(h)	Notts Co	D	1-1	Shoulder	17,272
3		23	(a)	Bolton W	L	0-4		11,835
4		30	(h)	Luton T	W	2-1	Koenan, Hibbitt	13,175
5	Sep	6	(h)	Cardiff C	W	2-1	Clarke, Shoulder (pen)	15,787
6		13	(a)	QPR	W	2-1	Hibbitt, Boam	10,865
7		20	(h)	Oldham Ath	D	0-0		19,786
8		27	(a)	Bristol R	D	0-0		5,171
9	Oct	4	(h)	West Ham U	D	0-0		24,866
10		7	(a)	Preston NE	W	3-2	Rafferty, Shinton 2	5,301
11		11	(a)	Bristol C	L	0-2		10,539
12		18	(h)	Swansea C	L	1-2	Rafferty	16,278
13		22	(h)	Shrewsbury T	W	1-0	Shinton	11,985
14		25	(a)	Chelsea	L	0-6		22,916
15	Nov	1	(h)	Watford	W	2-1	Hibbitt, Shinton	14,590
16		8	(a)	Cambridge U	L	1-2	Shinton	5,684
17		11	(a)	Notts Co	D	0-0		8,093
18		15	(h)	Sheffield W	W	1-0	Shinton	19,145
19		22	(h)	Wrexham	L	0-1		15,941
20		29	(a)	Orient	D	1-1	Shinton	5,800
21	Dec	13	(a)	Swansea C	L	0-4		11,672
22		20	(h)	Bristol C	D	0-0		14,131
23		26	(a)	Grimsby T	D	0-0		17,623
24		27	(h)	Derby Co	L	0-2		20,886
25	Jan	10	(a)	Wrexham	D	0-0		6,437
26		17	(a)	Luton T	W	1-0	Harford	10,774
27		31	(h)	Bolton W	W	2-1	Clarke, Martin	19,143
28	Feb	7	(h)	QPR	W	1-0	Waddle	20,404
29		21	(h)	Bristol R	D	0-0		14,364
30		25	(a)	Cardiff C	L	0-1		4,235
31		28	(a)	Oldham Ath	D	0-0		5,887
32	Mar	7	(a)	West Ham U	L	0-1		26,274
33		14	(h)	Preston NE	W	2-0	Harford 2	12,015
34		21	(a)	Shrewsbury T	L	0-1		4,975
35		28	(h)	Chelsea	W	1-0	Halliday	17,297
36	Apr	4	(h)	Watford	D	0-0		10,986
37		11	(h)	Cambridge U	W	2-1	Shoulder, (og)	11,013
38		15	(h)	Blackburn R	D	0-0		13,128
39		18	(a)	Derby Co	L	0-2		14,139
40		20	(h)	Grimsby T	D	1-1	Shoulder	13,170
41		25	(a)	Blackburn R	L	0-3		10,609
42	May	2	(h)	Orient	W	3-1	Walker, Harford, Trewick	11,639

FINAL LEAGUE POSITION : 11th in Division Two

Appearances

Sub. Appearances

Goals

Carr	Kelly	Davies	Cartwright	Boam	Carney	Rafferty	Shinton	Clarke	Wharton	Koenan	Barton	Halliday	Hardwick	Harford	Hibbitt	Johnson	Martin	Mitchell	Nicholson	Shoulder	Trewick	Waddle	Brownlie	Walker	Withe	
1	2	3	4	5	6	7	8	9	10	11																1
1	2	3	12	5		7	8*	9	10	11	6									4						2
1	2	3	12	5		7	8	9	10	11*	6									4						3
		3		5	2	9			12	11	6*		1	10				8		7			4			4
		3		5	2	8		9		11			1	10				6		7			4			5
		3	12	5	2	8		9		11			1	10*				6		7			4			6
		3		5	2	8		9		11			1	10				6		7			4			7
1	2	3		5	6	8		9		11				10						7			4			8
1	2	3		5		10		9		11				8				6		7			4			9
1	2	3		5		10		9		11				8				6		7			4			10
1	2	3	12	5		10		9						8	11		4	6		7*						11
1	2	3		5		10		9						8	11		4	6		7						12
1				5	2	10	7		8						11		4	6				9		3		13
1		8		5	2	10	7		11	12	6						4					9*		3		14
1				5	2	7	9	8							11	3	4	6		10						15
1				5	2	7	9	8							11	3	4	6		10						16
1				5	2	7	9	8							11	3	4	6		10						17
1				5	2	7	9	8							11	3	4	6		10						18
1				5	2	7	9	8							11	3	4	6		10						19
1				5	2		9	7	8						11	3	4	6		10						20
1		9		5	2			7	8	11*						3	4	6	12	10						21
1				5	2		7								11	3	4	6		10	8	9				22
1				5	2		7		10			9				3	4	6			8	11				23
1				5	2		7		10			9		12		3	4	6*			8	11				24
1				5	2		7		10		6	9				3	4				8	11				25
1				5	2		7		10		6	9				3	4				8	11				26
1				5	2		7	9	10		6					3	4				8	11				27
1				5	2		7	9	10		6			12		3	4*				8	11				28
1				5	4				10		6	9				3				7	8	11	2			29
1		7	4	5					10*		6	9				3					8	11	2	12		30
1		3		5	12				10		6	9					4			7	8	11*	2			31
1		3			12				10			5		6		9	4			7	8	11*	2			32
1		3							10			5		6		9	4			7	8		2	11		33
1		3			12				10			5*		6		9	4			7	8		2	11		34
1		3			12				10			5		6		9	4*			7	8		2	11		35
1		3							10			5		6		9	4			7	8		2	11		36
1		3							10			5		6		9	4			7	8		2	11		37
1		3							10			5		6		9	4			7	8		2	11		38
1		3							10			5		6		9	4			7	8		2	11		39
1		3							10			5		6		9	4			7	8		2	11		40
1		3							10			5		6		9	4			7	8		2	11		41
1		3							10			5		6		9	4			7	8		2	11		42
38	8	25	4	31	23	15	23	14	35	11	14	19	4	18	15	16	31	18	1	32	21	13	14	17	2	
			4		4						1	1							1					1		
		1		2	7	2		1			1			4	3		1			4	1	1		1	1	

1981-82

#	Month	Date		Opponent	Result	Score	Scorers	Attendance
1	Aug	29	(h)	Watford	L	0-1		19,244
2	Sep	5	(a)	QPR	L	0-3		14,176
3		12	(h)	Cambridge U	W	1-0	Trewick	14,666
4		19	(a)	Norwich C	L	1-2	Waddle	14,384
5		23	(h)	Shrewsbury T	W	2-0	Wharton, Shinton	13,783
6		26	(h)	Orient	W	1-0	Trewick	13,737
7		29	(a)	Bolton W	L	0-1		6,429
8	Oct	3	(a)	Cardiff C	W	4-0	Varadi 3, Davies (pen)	5,764
9		10	(h)	Derby Co	W	3-0	Wharton, Varadi 2	17,224
10		17	(a)	Barnsley	L	0-1		18,477
11		24	(h)	Rotherham U	D	1-1	Shinton	19,052
12		31	(a)	Oldham Ath	L	1-3	Davies	9,010
13	Nov	7	(a)	Chelsea	L	1-2	Waddle	16,509
14		14	(h)	Charlton Ath	W	4-1	Wharton, Varadi 2, Brown	15,254
15		21	(h)	Luton T	W	3-2	Varadi, Brown 2	21,084
16		24	(a)	Orient	L	0-1		4,026
17		28	(a)	Grimsby T	D	1-1	Wharton	9,256
18	Dec	5	(h)	Blackburn R	D	0-0		18,775
19	Jan	16	(a)	Watford	W	3-2	Varadi, Todd 2	12,333
20		30	(h)	Norwich C	W	2-1	Varadi, Mills	14,492
21	Feb	3	(h)	Bolton W	W	2-0	Wharton, Trewick (pen)	14,714
22		6	(a)	Cambridge U	L	0-1		5,092
23		13	(h)	Cardiff C	W	2-1	Varadi, Trewick	15,129
24		20	(a)	Shrewsbury T	D	0-0		4,636
25		24	(h)	Sheffield W	W	1-0	Varadi	19,174
26		27	(a)	Derby Co	D	2-2	Waddle, Varadi	12,257
27	Mar	3	(a)	Leicester C	L	0-3		12,497
28		6	(h)	Barnsley	W	1-0	Varadi	18,784
29		13	(a)	Rotherham U	D	0-0		16,905
30		20	(h)	Oldham Ath	W	2-0	Mills, Brownlie	18,531
31		27	(h)	Chelsea	W	1-0	Waddle	26,994
32		31	(h)	Crystal Palace	D	0-0		22,151
33	Apr	3	(a)	Charlton Ath	W	1-0	Waddle	6,357
34		6	(a)	Wrexham	L	2-4	Varadi 2	4,517
35		10	(h)	Leicester C	D	0-0		25,777
36		12	(a)	Sheffield W	L	1-2	Barton	29,917
37		17	(a)	Luton T	L	2-3	Mills, Trewick (pen)	13,041
38		24	(h)	Grimsby T	L	0-1		14,065
39	May	1	(a)	Blackburn R	L	1-4	Varadi	5,207
40		5	(h)	QPR	L	0-4		10,748
41		8	(h)	Wrexham	W	4-2	Waddle, Varadi, Trewick (pen), Brownlie	9,419
42		15	(a)	Crystal Palace	W	2-1	Waddle, Mills (pen)	8,453

FINAL LEAGUE POSITION : 9th in Division Two

Appearances

Sub. Appearances

Goals

Carr	Brownlie	Davies	Trewick	Barton	Halliday	Walker	Shoulder	Varadi	Wharton	Waddle	Martin	Bell	Brown	Carney	Ferris	Haddock	Cartwright	Mills	Pugh	Saunders	Shinton	Todd	#
1	2	3	4	5	6*	7	8	9	10	11	12												1
1		3	4	5	6	7	8	9	10*	11	12			2									2
1	2	3	4	5	6	7		9	10	11	8												3
1	2	3	4	5*	6	7		9	10	11	8		12										4
1	2	3	4	5	6		12	9*	10	11	8										7		5
1	2	3	4	5	6			9	10	11	8										7		6
1	2	3	4	5	6			9	10	11	8										7		7
1	2	3	4	5	6			9	10*	11	8					12					7		8
1	2	3	4	5	6			9	10	11*	8										7	12	9
1	2	3	4	5	6			9	10	11	8										7		10
1	2	3	4	5	6		12	9	10*	11	8										7		11
1	2	3*	4	5				9	10	11	8			6		12					7		12
1	2			4				9*	10	11	8		7	5		6			12	3			13
1	2	4						9	10	11	8		7	5		6				3			14
1	2	4					12	9	10	11	8		7*	5		6				3			15
1	2	4					7	9	10	11	8			5		6				3			16
1	2	4						9	10	11	8		7	5		6				3			17
1	2	4					12	9	10	11	8		7*	5		6				3			18
1	2	4						9	10	11	8			5		6				3		7	19
1	2	4						9	10	11	8			5		6		7		3			20
1		4	5					9	10	11	8			2		6		7		3			21
1		4*	5					9	10	11	8			2		6		7		3	12		22
1	2	4	5					9	10	11	8					6		7		3			23
1	2	4						9	10	11	8*			5		6	12	7		3			24
1	2	4						9	10	11				5		6	8	7		3			25
1	2	4						9	10	11				5		6	8	7		3			26
1	2	4						9	10	11				5		6	8	7		3			27
1	2	4					12	9		11	8			5		6	10	7*		3			28
1	2	4						9		11	8			5		6	10	7		3			29
1	2	4					12	9		11	8			5		6*	10	7		3			30
1	2	4						9		11	8			5		6	10	7		3			31
1	2	4						9		11	8			5		6	10	7		3			32
1	2	4						9		11	8			5		6	10	7		3			33
1	2	4*						9	12	11	8			5		6	10	7		3			34
1	2	4	5				12	9		11	8*			6			10	7		3			35
1	2	4	5					9		11	8			6			10	7		3			36
1	2	4	5*					9	12	11	8			6			10	7		3			37
1	2	4						9	12	11	8			5			10	7		3*			38
1	2	3						9	10	11*	8	4		5	12	6		7					39
1	2	4*						9		11	8	10		5	12	6		7		3			40
1	2	4	5	6				9	12	11	8						10	7		3*			41
1		4*	5	6				9	12	11	8					2	10	7		3			42
42	38	13	40	20	13	5	3	42	28	42	37	2	5	27		28	16	23		29	8	1	
							7		5		2			1	2	2	1		1		1	1	
	2	2	6	1				18	5	7			3			4				2	2		

1982-83

1	Aug	28	(h)	QPR	W	1-0	Keegan	35,718
2	Sep	1	(a)	Blackburn R	W	2-1	Keegan, Martin	14,421
3		4	(a)	Bolton W	L	1-3	Keegan (pen)	17,707
4		8	(h)	Middlesbrough	D	1-1	Channon	27,984
5		11	(h)	Chelsea	D	1-1	Clarke	29,136
6		18	(a)	Shrewsbury T	L	1-2	Varadi	7,907
7		25	(h)	Barnsley	L	1-2	Varadi	24,522
8	Oct	2	(a)	Rotherham U	W	5-1	Todd, Keegan 4 (1 pen)	12,436
9		9	(a)	Oldham Ath	D	2-2	Varadi 2	9,000
10		16	(h)	Fulham	L	1-4	Keegan (pen)	29,647
11		23	(h)	Crystal Palace	W	1-0	Waddle	22,616
12		30	(a)	Leeds U	L	1-3	Anderson	26,570
13	Nov	6	(h)	Burnley	W	3-0	Waddle, Varadi, Keegan	20,961
14		13	(a)	Leicester C	D	2-2	Keegan 2	15,044
15		20	(a)	Carlisle U	L	0-2		16,276
16		27	(h)	Cambridge U	W	2-0	McDermott, Martin	20,385
17	Dec	4	(a)	Charlton Ath	L	0-2		10,381
18		11	(h)	Wolverhampton W	D	1-1	Wharton	19,595
19		18	(a)	Sheffield W	D	1-1	Varadi	16,310
20		27	(h)	Derby Co	W	1-0	Gayle	30,558
21		28	(a)	Grimsby T	D	2-2	Varadi, Gayle	14,983
22	Jan	1	(h)	Carlisle U	D	2-2	Keegan 2	28,578
23		3	(h)	Bolton W	D	2-2	Waddle, Martin	23,533
24		15	(a)	QPR	L	0-2		13,972
25		22	(h)	Shrewsbury R	W	4-0	Wharton 2, Varadi, Keegan (pen)	19,333
26	Feb	5	(a)	Middlesbrough	D	1-1	Keegan	25,184
27		19	(h)	Oldham Ath	W	1-0	McDermott	20,689
28		26	(a)	Fulham	D	2-2	McDermott, Varadi	14,277
29	Mar	5	(a)	Crystal Palace	W	2-0	Waddle, Varadi	10,239
30		12	(h)	Leeds U	W	2-1	Waddle, Keegan (pen)	24,543
31		19	(a)	Burnley	L	0-1		13,900
32		26	(h)	Leicester C	D	2-2	McDermott, Keegan	22,692
33	Apr	2	(h)	Grimsby T	W	4-0	Varadi 2, McDonald, Keegan	20,202
34		4	(a)	Derby Co	L	1-2	Waddle	19,779
35		9	(h)	Blackburn R	W	3-2	Waddle, Varadi, (og)	17,839
36		16	(a)	Chelsea	W	2-0	Varadi, Keegan (pen)	13,446
37		20	(h)	Rotherham U	W	4-0	McDermott, Varadi, Keegan, Wharton	18,523
38		23	(h)	Charlton Ath	W	4-2	McDermott, Varadi 2, Wharton	20,567
39		30	(a)	Cambridge U	L	0-1		7,591
40	May	4	(a)	Barnsley	W	5-0	Varadi 2, McDonald 2, Keegan	10,958
41		7	(h)	Sheffield W	W	2-1	Varadi, (og)	29,874
42		14	(a)	Wolverhampton W	D	2-2	Varadi, McDonald	22,446

FINAL LEAGUE POSITION : 5th in Division Two

Appearances

Sub. Appearances

Goals

Hardwick	Craggs	Saunders	Trewick	Clarke	Haddock	Keegan	Martin	Varadi	Cartwright	Waddle	Wharton	McCreery	McDermott	McDonald	Thomas	Anderson	Bell	Carney	Carr	Channon	Todd	Ferris	Gayle	Hedworth	
1	2	3	4*	5	6	7	8	9	10	11	12														1
1	2	3		5	6	7	4	9	8	11*	10					12									2
1	2	3		5	6	7	4	9	8	11	10														3
1	2	3		5	6	7	4	9	10	11										8					4
1	2	3		5	6	7	4	9		11*	10						12			8					5
1	2	3		5	6	7	4	9			10			12		11*				8					6
1	2	3		5	6	7	4*	9			10			11						8	12				7
		3		5		7	4	9		11	10					2		6	1	8					8
		3		5		7	4	9			12	11	10			2		6	1	8*					9
		3		5		7	4	9			12	11	10			2		6	1	8*					10
		3		5	6	7	4	9		11	10	8				2			1						11
					6	7	4	9*		11	3	8	10			2		5	1				12		12
					6	7	4*	9		11	3	8	10	12		2		5	1						13
					6	7	4	9		11	3	8	10			2		5	1						14
	12			5		4		9		11	3	8	10			2		6	1		7*				15
	12			5			4	9*		11	3	8	10			2			1			7	6		16
				5			4			11	3	8	10			2		12	1		7*	9	6		17
				5			4			9	3	8	10	11		2			1			7	6		18
				5	6			9		11	3	8	10	4		2*		12	1			7			19
	2			5	6	7		9		11	3	4	10						1			8			20
				5	6	7	12	9		11	3	4*	10			2			1			8			21
	2			5	6	7	12	9		11	3	4*	10						1			8			22
				5	6	7	4			9	3	11*	10	12		2			1			8			23
				5		7	4	9*		11	3		10	8		2		6	1				12		24
		3		5		7*	4	9		11	10			8		2		6	1				12		25
		3		5		7	4	9		11	10			8		2		6	1						26
				5		7	4	9		11*	3		10	8		2		6	1				12		27
				5		7	4	9		11	3		10	8		2		6	1						28
				5		7	4	9		11	3		10	8		2		6	1						29
				5		7	4	9		11	3		10	8		2		6	1						30
				5		7	4	9		11	3		10	8		2		6	1						31
				5		7	4	9		11	3	12	10	8*		2		6	1						32
				5		7	4	9		11	3	12	10*	8		2		6	1						33
				5		7	4*	9		11	3	12	10	8		2		6	1						34
				5		7		9*		11	3	4	10	8		2		6	1				12		35
				5		7		9		11	3	4	10	8		2		6	1						36
				5		7	12	9		11*	3	4	10	8		2		6	1						37
				5		7	12	9		11	3	4	10	8		2*		6	1						38
	2			5		7	12	9		11	3	4	10	8*				6	1						39
				5		7		9		11	3	4	10	8	1	2		6							40
				5		7		9		11	3	4	10	8	1	2		6							41
				5		7	12	9		11	3	4	10	8*	1	2		6							42
7	10	13	1	39	17	37	29	39	4	37	38	23	32	22	3	31	1	27	32	4	4	1	8	3	
	2						6			3	3			2		2	1	2			1	4	1		
				1		21	3	21		7	5		6	4		1					1	1	2		

41

1983-84

1	Aug	27	(a)	Leeds U	W	1-0	Anderson	30,806
2		29	(h)	Shrewsbury T	L	0-1		29,123
3	Sep	3	(h)	Oldham A	W	3-0	McDermott, Waddle, Mills	22,644
4		6	(a)	Middlesbrough	L	2-3	Keegan, Mills	19,648
5		10	(a)	Grimsby T	D	1-1	Keegan	9,000
6		17	(h)	Crystal Palace	W	3-1	Ryan, Waddle, Keegan	22,774
7		24	(a)	Barnsley	D	1-1	Waddle	14,085
8	Oct	1	(h)	Portsmouth	W	4-2	Waddle 2, Keegan (pen), Wharton	25,411
9		8	(h)	Charlton A	W	2-1	Keegan 2	23,247
10		16	(a)	Swansea C	W	2-1	Wharton, Mills	9,807
11		19	(a)	Cardiff C	W	2-0	Keegan, Beardsley	9,926
12		29	(h)	Manchester C	W	5-0	Beardsley 3, Keegan, Waddle	33,588
13	Nov	5	(h)	Fulham	W	3-2	Keegan, Mills, Wharton	31,568
14		12	(a)	Chelsea	L	0-4		30,628
15		19	(a)	Sheffield W	L	2-4	McDermott, Keegan (pen)	41,134
16		26	(h)	Cambridge U	W	2-1	Keegan (pen), Beardsley	25,005
17	Dec	3	(a)	Derby Co	L	2-3	Keegan, Waddle	18,691
18		10	(h)	Huddersfield T	W	5-2	Keegan, Beardsley, Waddle 2, McDermott	25,652
19		17	(a)	Brighton & HA	W	1-0	Waddle	13,896
20		26	(h)	Blackburn R	D	1-1	Waddle	33,802
21		27	(a)	Carlisle U	L	1-3	Waddle	14,756
22		31	(a)	Oldham A	W	2-1	Keegan 2	8,518
23	Jan	2	(h)	Barnsley	W	1-0	Waddle	29,833
24		21	(a)	Crystal Palace	L	1-3	Beardsley	9,464
25	Feb	4	(a)	Portsmouth	W	4-1	Keegan 2, Beardsley 2	18,686
26		11	(h)	Grimsby T	L	0-1		28,526
27		18	(a)	Manchester C	W	2-1	Beardsley, Keegan	41,767
28		25	(h)	Cardiff C	W	3-1	Waddle, Keegan 2 (1 pen)	27,909
29	Mar	3	(a)	Fulham	D	2-2	Beardsley, Keegan	12,290
30		10	(h)	Chelsea	D	1-1	McDermott	36,506
31		17	(h)	Middlesbrough	W	3-1	Beardsley, McDermott, Keegan	30,386
32		24	(a)	Shrewsbury T	D	2-2	Johnson (og), Keegan	8,313
33		28	(h)	Leeds U	W	1-0	Irwin (og)	30,877
34		31	(h)	Swansea C	W	2-0	Wharton, Beardsley	27,308
35	Apr	7	(a)	Charlton A	W	3-1	Waddle, McDermott, Beardsley	15,289
36		14	(h)	Sheffield W	L	0-1		36,725
37		20	(a)	Blackburn R	D	1-1	Trewick	19,196
38		23	(h)	Carlisle U	W	5-1	Keegan 2, Waddle, Beardsley 2	33,386
39		28	(a)	Cambridge U	L	0-1		7,720
40	May	5	(h)	Derby Co	W	4-0	Keegan, Beardsley 2, Waddle	35,850
41		7	(a)	Huddersfield T	D	2-2	Beardsley, Mills	25,101
42		12	(h)	Brighton & HA	W	3-1	Keegan, Waddle, Beardsley	36,415

FINAL LEAGUE POSITION: 3rd in Division Two

Appearances

Sub Appearances

Goals

Carr	Anderson	Ryan	McCreery	Clarke	Carney	Keegan	McDonald	Mills	McDermott	Waddle	Wharton	Thomas	Trewick	Beardsley	Saunders	Haddock	Roeder	
1*	2	3	4	5	6	7	8	9	10	11	12							1
	2	3	4	5	6	7	8*	9	10	11	12	1						2
	2	3	4	5	6	7	8	9	10	11		1						3
	2	3	4	5	6	7	8*	9	10	11	12	1						4
	2	3	4	5	6	7		9	10	11	8	1						5
	2	3	4	5	6	7		9	10	11	8*	1	12					6
	2	3	4	5*	6	7		9	10	11	8	1		12				7
	2	3	4		6	7	12	10	9*	11		1		8	5			8
	2	3	4		6	7	12	10	9	11*		1		8	5			9
	2	3	4		6	7	12	10	11*	8		1		9	5			10
	2	3	4		6	7		10	9	11		1		8	5			11
	2	3	4		6	7		10	9	11		1		8	5			12
	2	3	4		6	7	12	10	9	11		1		8	5			13
	2	3	4*		6	7	12	10	9	11		1		8	5			14
	2	3			6	7	4	10	9	11		1		8	5			15
	2	3			6	7	4	10	9	11		1		8	5			16
		3	4*		6	7	12	10	9	11		1		8	5	2		17
	2	3*	4		6	7	12	10	9	11		1		8	5			18
	2		4		6	7	11	10	9	3		1		8	5			19
	2		4			7	12	11*	10	9	3	1		8	5		6	20
	2		4	11		7		10	9	3		1		8	5		6	21
	2	3	4			7	8		10	9*	11	1	12		5		6	22
	2	3	4			7			10	9	11	1		8	5		6	23
1	2	3	4	5		7			10	9	11			8			6	24
1	2	11*	4	5	12	7			10	9	3			8			6	25
1	2		4	5		7	11		10	9	3			8			6	26
1	2		4	5		7			10	9	3		11	8			6	27
1	2		4	5		7			10	9	3		11	8			6	28
	2		4	5		7			10	9	3	1	11	8			6	29
1	2		4	5		7			10	9	3		11	8			6	30
1	2		4		5	7			10	9	3		11	8			6	31
1	2		4		5	7			10	9	3		11	8			6	32
1	2		4		5	7			10	9	3		11	8			6	33
1	2		4		5	7			10	9	3		11	8			6	34
1	2		4		5	7			10	9	3		11	8			6	35
1	2		4		5	7			10	9	3		11	8			6	36
1	2		4		5	7			10	9	3		11*	8		12	6	37
1	2		4		5	7	11		10	9	3			8			6	38
1	2		4		5	7	11*		10	9	3			8		12	6	39
1	2		4		5	7			10	9	3		11	8			6	40
1	2		4	5			8		10	9	3		11	7			6	41
1	2		4	5		7			10	9	3		11	8			6	42
19	41	22	40	14	32	41	10	10	42	42	38	23	14	34	16	1	23	
				1			2	6			3		2	1		2		
		1	1		27		5	6	18	4			1	20				

1984-85

1	Aug	25	(a)	Leicester C	W	3-2	Carney, McCreery, Waddle	18,636
2		27	(h)	Sheffield W	W	2-1	Beardsley (pen), Wharton	29,700
3	Sep	1	(h)	Aston Villa	W	3-0	Beardsley, Waddle 2	31,497
4		4	(a)	Arsenal	L	0-2		37,078
5		8	(a)	Manchester U	L	0-5		54,915
6		15	(h)	Everton	L	2-3	Beardsley (pen), Wharton	26,944
7		22	(a)	QPR	D	5-5	McDonald, Waddle 3, Wharton	14,144
8		29	(h)	West Ham U	D	1-1	Beardsley	29,452
9	Oct	6	(a)	Ipswich T	W	3-0	Burley (og), Heard, Waddle	25,094
10		13	(a)	Coventry C	D	1-1	Beardsley (pen)	14,091
11		20	(h)	Nottingham F	D	1-1	Wharton	28,252
12		27	(a)	Watford	D	3-3	Beardsley, McDonald, Wharton	18,753
13	Nov	3	(a)	Luton T	D	2-2	Beardsley, Heard	10,009
14		10	(h)	Chelsea	W	2-1	McDonald, Waddle	23,723
15		18	(h)	Liverpool	L	0-2		28,003
16		24	(a)	Southampton	L	0-1		18,895
17	Dec	1	(h)	Stoke C	W	2-1	Anderson (pen), Waddle	21,135
18		8	(a)	Tottenham H	L	1-3	Waddle	29,695
19		15	(h)	Norwich C	D	1-1	Waddle	20,030
20		22	(a)	Aston Villa	L	0-4		14,491
21		26	(a)	West Brom A	L	1-2	Baird	20,405
22		29	(h)	Arsenal	L	1-3	Beardsley (pen)	27,349
23	Jan	1	(h)	Sunderland	W	3-1	Beardsley 3 (1 pen)	36,821
24		12	(a)	Everton	L	0-4		32,156
25	Feb	2	(a)	West Ham U	D	1-1	Waddle	17,723
26		9	(h)	Manchester U	D	1-1	Beardsley	31,798
27		16	(a)	Chelsea	L	0-1		21,826
28		23	(h)	Luton T	W	1-0	Wharton	23,737
29	Mar	2	(h)	Watford	W	3-1	Cunningham, Megson, Reilly	24,923
30		9	(a)	Nottingham F	D	0-0		17,425
31		20	(h)	Leicester C	L	1-4	Beardsley	21,967
32		23	(a)	Ipswich T	D	1-1	McDonald	14,366
33		30	(a)	Sheffield W	L	2-4	Beardsley (pen), Waddle	26,525
34	Apr	6	(h)	West Brom A	W	1-0	Beardsley	22,690
35		8	(a)	Sunderland	D	0-0		28,246
36		13	(h)	QPR	W	1-0	Reilly	21,711
37		17	(h)	Coventry C	L	0-1		19,578
38		20	(a)	Liverpool	L	1-3	McDonald	34,733
39		27	(h)	Southampton	W	2-1	Reilly, Wharton	20,871
40	May	4	(a)	Stoke C	W	1-0	Dyson (og)	7,088
41		6	(h)	Tottenham H	L	2-3	Beardsley 2 (2 pens)	29,702
42		11	(a)	Norwich C	D	0-0		18,399

FINAL LEAGUE POSITION: 14th in Division One

Appearances

Sub Appearances

Goals

Carr	Brown	Ryan	Carney	Roeder	Saunders	McDonald	Wharton	Waddle	Beardsley	McCreery	Anderson	Ferris	Haddock	Heard	Hedworth	Clarke	Megson	Allon	Baird	Thomas	Cunningham	Reilly	Gascoigne	
1	2	3	4	5	6	7	8	9	10	11														1
1	2	3	4	5	6	7	8	9	10	11*	12													2
1	2	3	4	5	6	7	8	9	10	11														3
1	2	3	4	5	6	7	8	9	10	11														4
1	2	3*	4	5	6	7	8	9	10	11	12													5
1	2	3	4*	5	6	7	8	9	10	11		12												6
1	2		6	3		7	8	9	10	11	5		4											7
1	2		6	3		7	8	9	10	11	5			4										8
1	2		6	3		7	8	9	10	11	5			4										9
1	2		6	3		7	8	9	10	11	5			4										10
1	2			3		7	8	9	10	11	5	12		4	6*									11
1	2			3		7	8	9	10	11	5			4			6							12
1	2			3		7	8	9	10	11	5			4			6							13
1	2			3		7	8	9*	10	11	5	12		4			6							14
1	2		6	3		7*	8	9	10	11	5	12		4										15
1	2		6	3		7	8	9	10*	11	5			4			12							16
1	2		6	3		12	8	9		11	5			4			7	10*						17
1	2		6	3		12	8	9	10	11	5			4*			7							18
1	2		6	3			8	9	10	11	5			4			7							19
1	2					8	11	9		4	5			3		6	7		10					20
1	2		4			11	8	9			5			3		6	7		10					21
1	2		6			8		9	10	11*	5			3		4	7		12					22
1	2			3		11	8		10		5			4		6	7		9					23
1	2		4	3		12	8	9		11	5*					6	7		10					24
	2			5		7	3	9	10	11				4		6	8			1				25
	2		6			4	3	9	10	11				5			7			1	8			26
	2		5			4	3	9	10	11*	12			10		6	7			1	8			27
	2		6				3	9	10	11				5			4			1	8	7		28
	2		6					9	10	11	3			5			4			1	8	7		29
	2		6					9	10	11	3			5			4			1	8	7		30
	2		6			12		9	10	11	3			5			4*			1	8	7		31
	2		6			7	12		10	11	3			5			4			1	8	9*		32
	2		6			12		9*	10	11	3			5			4			1	8	7		33
	2		6			12			10	11	3			5		7*	4			1	8	9		34
	2		6			7			10	11	3			5			4			1	8	9		35
	2		6			7	3		10	11	5						4			1	8	9*	12	36
	2		6			12	3		10	11	5					7	4			1	8*	9		37
	2		6			12	3	9	10	11	5					7*	4			1	8			38
	2*		6			7	3	9	10	11	12			5			4			1	8			39
	2		6			7	3	9	10	11				5			4			1	8			40
	2		6			7	3	9	10	11				5			4*			1	8		12	41
	2		6			7	3	9	10	11				5			4			1	8			42
24	39	6	6	36	21	29	35	35	38	34	31		1	34	1	23	19	1	4	18	13	14		
						7		1		1	4	4					1	1				2		
		1				5	7	13	17	1	1			2			1		1		1	3		

45

1	Aug	17	(a)	Southampton	D	1-1	Beardsley (pen)	16,401
2		21	(h)	Luton T	D	2-2	Beardsley, Roeder	21,304
3		24	(h)	Liverpool	W	1-0	Reilly	29,670
4		26	(a)	Coventry C	W	2-1	Reilly, Stewart	12,097
5		31	(h)	QPR	W	3-1	McDonald, Reilly, Beardsley	25,026
6	Sep	4	(a)	Manchester U	L	0-3		51,102
7		7	(a)	Tottenham H	L	1-5	Davies	23,883
8		14	(h)	WBA	W	4-1	McDonald, Clarke, Reilly 2	21,855
9		21	(h)	Oxford U	W	3-0	Beardsley, McDonald, Gascoigne	23,596
10		28	(a)	Arsenal	D	0-0		24,104
11	Oct	5	(h)	West Ham U	L	1-2	Reilly	26,709
12		12	(a)	Ipswich T	D	2-2	Beardsley, McDonald	12,536
13		19	(h)	Nottingham F	L	0-3		23,151
14		26	(a)	Aston Villa	W	2-1	Gascoigne, Beardsley	12,633
15	Nov	2	(h)	Watford	D	1-1	Gascoigne	20,649
16		9	(a)	Birmingham C	W	1-0	Reilly	8,162
17		16	(h)	Chelsea	L	1-3	Roeder	22,355
18		23	(a)	Manchester C	L	0-1		25,179
19		30	(h)	Leicester C	W	2-1	Clarke, Beardsley	17,304
20	Dec	7	(a)	Luton T	L	0-2		10,319
21		14	(h)	Southampton	W	2-1	Roeder, Beardsley	19,229
22		21	(a)	Liverpool	D	1-1	Beardsley	30,746
23		26	(a)	Sheffield W	D	2-2	Roeder, Beardsley	30,269
24	Jan	1	(h)	Everton	D	2-2	Gascoigne, Beardsley	27,820
25		11	(a)	West Brom A	D	1-1	Wharton	9,100
26		18	(a)	QPR	L	1-3	Gascoigne	13,159
27	Feb	1	(h)	Coventry C	W	3-2	Beardsley, Allon, Wharton	16,637
28		8	(a)	Nottingham F	W	2-1	Beardsley 2	15,388
29	Mar	1	(h)	Arsenal	W	1-0	Roeder	21,860
30		15	(h)	Ipswich T	W	3-1	Beardsley, Whitehurst, Gascoigne	18,851
31		19	(a)	Oxford U	W	2-1	Gascoigne, Beardsley	10,052
32		22	(h)	Tottenham H	D	2-2	Whitehurst, Anderson	30,615
33		29	(a)	Everton	L	0-1		41,116
34		31	(h)	Sheffield W	W	4-1	Stephenson, Gascoigne, Beardsley, Whitehurst	25,614
35	Apr	5	(a)	Watford	L	1-4	McClelland (og)	14,706
36		9	(h)	Aston Villa	D	2-2	Whitehurst, Gascoigne	20,107
37		12	(h)	Birmingham C	W	4-1	Beardsley 2, Anderson, Whitehurst	19,981
38		16	(h)	Manchester U	L	2-4	Stewart, Cunningham	31,840
39		19	(a)	Chelsea	D	1-1	Anderson	18,970
40		21	(a)	West Ham U	L	1-8	Whitehurst	24,735
41		26	(h)	Manchester C	W	3-1	Clarke, Roeder, Whitehurst	22,689
42	May	3	(a)	Leicester C	L	0-2		13,171

FINAL LEAGUE POSITION: 11th in Division One

Appearances

Sub Appearances

Goals

Thomas	Anderson	Wharton	Davies	Clarke	Roeder	McDonald	Megson	Reilly	Beardsley	Gascoigne	McCreery	Stewart	McKinnon	Hedworth	Haddock	Cunningham	Bailey	Allon	Whitehurst	Stephenson	McKellar	No.
1	2	3	4	5	6	7	8	9	10	11*	12											1
1	2	3		5	6	7	8*	9	10	4	12	11										2
1	2	3		5	6	7		9	10	4	8	11										3
1	2	3		5	6	7		9	10	4	8	11										4
1	2	3		5	6	7	12	9	10	4	8	11*										5
1	2	3		5	6	7		9	10	4	8	11										6
1	2		4	5	6	7		9	10	12	8	11	3*									7
1	3		4	5	6	7		9	10	12	8*	11		2								8
1	3		4	5	6	7		9	10	12	8	11		2*								9
1	3		4	5	6	7			10		8	11			2	9						10
1	3		4	5	6	7		9	10		8	11		2								11
1	3		4	5	6	7		9	10		8	11		2								12
1	3		4	5	6	7		9	10		8	11			2*	12						13
1	2			5	6	7	12	9*	10	8	4	11					3					14
1	2			5	6	7*		9	10	11	4	12				8	3					15
1	3	2		5	6	12		9	10	7	4	11*						8				16
1	2	11		5	6			9	10	7	4*	12					3	8				17
1	2	11	7	5	6	12		9	10	8*	4						3					18
1	4	8	2	5	6	7			10			11				9	3					19
1	7	8	2	5	6				10		4	11					3		9			20
1	2	11	8	5	6				10		4						3		9	7		21
1	2			5	6				10	8	4	11					3		9	7		22
1	2			5	6				10	8	4	11					3		9	7		23
1	2			5	6				10	8	4	11					3		9	7		24
1	2	11		5	6				10	8	4						3		9	7		25
1	2	11		5	6	12			10	8	4						3		9	7*		26
1	2	11		5	6	12			10	8*	4						3	9		7		27
1	2*	11		5	6	12			10	8	4					9	3			7		28
1	2	11		5	6				10*	8	4					12	3		9	7		29
	2			5	6	11*			10	8	4					12	3		9	7	1	30
	2			5	6				10	8	4					11	3		9	7	1	31
	2			5	6				10	8	4					11	3		9	7	1	32
	2			5	6				10	8	4	11					3		9	7	1	33
	2			5	6				10	8	4	11*				12	3		9	7	1	34
	2			5	6				10	8	4	11*				12	3		9	7	1	35
				5	6				10	8	4	11*			2	12	3		9	7	1	36
1	2			5	6	11			10	8	4						3		9	7		37
1				5	6	2			10	8*	4	11				12	3		9	7		38
	8			5	6	2			10		4					11	3		9	7	1	39
1*	5				6	2			10		4	12			8	11	3		9	7		40
				5	6	2			10		4				8	11	3		9	7	1	41
				5	6	2			10		4	11			8	9	3			7	1	42
32	38	15	14	41	42	23	2	17	42	28	39	25	1	4	6	10	28	3	20	22	10	
						5	2			3	2	3				7						
	3	2	1	3	6	4		7	19	9	2					1		1	7	1		

47

1986-87

1	Aug	23	(h)	Liverpool	L	0-2		33,306
2		25	(a)	Tottenham H	D	1-1	Beardsley	25,381
3		30	(a)	Luton T	D	0-0		9,254
4	Sep	3	(h)	QPR	L	0-2		23,080
5		6	(h)	Sheffield W	L	2-3	Allon, Scott	22,010
6		13	(a)	Coventry C	L	0-3		11,370
7		20	(h)	Wimbledon	W	1-0	Gascoigne	21,545
8		27	(a)	Norwich C	L	0-2		15,735
9	Oct	4	(a)	Southampton	L	1-4	Thomas A.	14,622
10		11	(h)	Manchester C	W	3-1	McDonald (pen), Gascoigne, Cunningham	21,780
11		18	(h)	Arsenal	L	1-2	Stewart	22,368
12		25	(a)	Aston Villa	L	0-2		14,614
13	Nov	1	(h)	Oxford U	D	0-0		19,622
14		8	(a)	Leicester C	D	1-1	McDonald (pen)	9,836
15		15	(h)	Watford	D	2-2	Anderson, McDonald (pen)	23,645
16		22	(a)	Chelsea	W	3-1	Thomas A. 2, Beardsley	14,544
17		30	(h)	West Ham U	W	4-0	McDonald, Thomas A. 2, Jackson D.	22,077
18	Dec	6	(a)	Charlton A	D	1-1	Goddard	7,333
19		13	(h)	Nottingham F	W	3-2	Wharton, Thomas A., Beardsley	26,191
20		21	(a)	Sheffield W	L	0-2		28,897
21		26	(h)	Everton	L	0-4		35,079
22		27	(a)	Watford	L	0-1		18,011
23	Jan	1	(a)	Manchester U	L	1-4	Jackson D.	43,334
24		3	(h)	Coventry C	L	1-2	McDonald	22,366
25		24	(a)	Liverpool	L	0-2		38,054
26	Feb	7	(h)	Luton T	D	2-2	Jackson P., Goddard	22,437
27		14	(a)	QPR	L	1-2	Goddard	10,731
28		28	(a)	Wimbledon	L	1-3	Beardsley	6,779
29	Mar	7	(h)	Aston Villa	W	2-1	Cunningham, Beardsley	21,224
30		21	(a)	Manchester C	D	0-0		23,060
31		25	(h)	Tottenham H	D	1-1	Goddard	30,782
32		28	(h)	Southampton	W	2-0	Goddard, Gascoigne	22,717
33	Apr	4	(h)	Leicester C	W	2-0	Wharton, Goddard	23,360
34		8	(h)	Norwich C	W	4-1	Goddard, Gascoigne, McDonald (pen), Jackson D.	24,534
35		11	(a)	Oxford U	D	1-1	Goddard	10,526
36		14	(a)	Arsenal	W	1-0	Goddard	17,353
37		18	(h)	Manchester U	W	2-1	Roeder, Goddard	32,706
38		20	(a)	Everton	L	0-3		43,593
39		25	(h)	Chelsea	W	1-0	Goddard	21,962
40	May	2	(a)	West Ham U	D	1-1	McDonald (pen)	17,844
41		4	(h)	Charlton A	L	0-3		26,950
42		9	(a)	Nottingham F	L	1-2	Gascoigne	17,788

FINAL LEAGUE POSITION: 17th in Division One

Appearances

Sub Appearances

Goals

48

Thomas M.	Anderson	Bailey	McCreery	Clarke	Roeder	Davies	Gascoigne	Whitehurst	Beardsley	Wharton	McDonald	Bogie	Allon	Stewart	Scott	Cunningham	Thomas A.	Kelly	Stephenson	Jackson D.	Jackson P.	Goddard	Nesbit	Wrightson	Craig	Tinnion	
1	2	3	4	5	6	7	8*	9	10	11	12																1
1	2	3	4	5	6	7		9	10	11	8																2
1	2	3	4		6		8	9	10	11	5	7															3
1	2	3	4		6	7	8	9		11*	5		10	12													4
1	2	3	4			7	8	9			5		10	11	6												5
1	6	3	4	5		7	8	9			2			11		10											6
	2	3	4	5	6		8	9			7			11			10	1									7
1	2*	3	4	5	6		12		10		11		9				8		7								8
1	6		4*	5			12	11	10	3	2		9				8		7								9
	6		4		5		8		10	3	2			11		9		1	7								10
	6				5		8		10	3	2			11*		9	4	1	7	12							11
1	3		4		6		12		10		2			11		9	8		7*		5						12
1	3		4		6	7*			10	12	2			11		9	8				5						13
1	2		4		6				10	3	7			11*		12	8				5	9					14
1	2		4		6				10	3	7					12	8*		11		5	9					15
1	2*		4		6				10	3	7						8		11	12	5	9					16
1	2		4		6				10	3	7						8		11	12	5	9*					17
1	2*		4		6				10	3	7						8			11	5	9	12				18
1			4		6				10	3	2						8		7	11*	5	9	12				19
1					6				10	3	2						8		7	11	5	9	4				20
1					6				10	3	2		12				8		7*	11	5	9		4			21
1					6				10	3	2						8		7	11	5	9		4			22
1			4		6				10	3	2		12				8		7*	11	5	9					23
1			4		6	2*				3	7		12				8			10	5	9		11			24
1	4				6				10	3	2			11			8		7		5	9					25
1		4*			6				10	3	2					8	7			12	5	9			11		26
1					6				10	3	2				4	8	7				5	9		11			27
1			6						10	3	2				4	8	7*				5	9		12	11		28
1	6		4						10	3	2	8*				9			7	12	5			11			29
1	11		4		6				10	3	2					9			7	12	5	8*					30
1	11		4		6		8		10	3	2					12			7		5	9					31
1	11		4		6		8		10	3	2								7		5	9					32
1	11		4		6		8		10	3	2	'							7		5	9					33
1	11		4*		6		8		10	3	2								7	12	5	9					34
1	11				6		8		10	3	2					12			7*	4	5	9					35
1	11				6		8		10	3	2					12			7	4	5	9*					36
1	11				6		8		10*	3	2					12			7	4	5	9					37
1					6		8			3	2		12				10		7*	4	5	9		11			38
1	11		4		6		8			3	2						10		7		5	9					39
1	11		4		6		8			3	2						10		7*		5	9			12		40
1	2				6		8			3							10	12	7	9	5				4*	11	41
1	2		4		6	12	8			3							9	10	7*	5						11	42
39	32	8	30	7	37	6	21	8	32	36	39	1	5	9	3	14	23	3	24	16	31	26	1	3	5	3	
						1	3			1	1			5		3	4		7					2	1	1	
	1		1				5	5	2	7		1	1	1		2	6		3	1	11						

49

1987-88

#	Month	Date		Opponent	Res	Score	Scorers	Attendance
1	Aug	19	(a)	Tottenham H	L	1-3	McCreery	26,261
2		22	(a)	Sheffield W	W	1-0	Jackson D.	22,031
3		29	(h)	Nottingham F	L	0-1		20,111
4	Sep	1	(a)	Norwich C	D	1-1	Jackson P.	16,636
5		5	(h)	Wimbledon	L	1-2	McDonald (pen)	22,684
6		12	(a)	Manchester U	D	2-2	Mirandinha 2	45,137
7		20	(h)	Liverpool	L	1-4	McDonald (pen)	24,141
8		26	(h)	Southampton	W	2-1	Mirandinha, Goddard	18,093
9	Oct	3	(a)	Chelsea	D	2-2	Goddard, Wharton	22,071
10		17	(h)	Everton	D	1-1	Mirandinha	20,266
11		24	(a)	Coventry C	W	3-1	Goddard, Gascoigne, Jackson D.	18,585
12		31	(h)	Arsenal	L	0-1		23,662
13	Nov	7	(a)	Luton T	L	0-4		7,638
14		14	(h)	Derby Co	D	0-0		21,698
15		21	(a)	QPR	D	1-1	Jackson P.	11,794
16		28	(h)	Charlton A	W	2-1	Cornwell, Mirandinha	19,453
17	Dec	5	(a)	Oxford U	W	3-1	McDonald (pen), O'Neill, Mirandinha	8,190
18		12	(h)	Portsmouth	D	1-1	Mirandinha	20,455
19		19	(a)	West Ham U	L	1-2	Mirandinha	18,679
20		26	(h)	Manchester U	W	1-0	Roeder	26,461
21		28	(a)	Liverpool	L	0-4		44,637
22	Jan	1	(a)	Nottingham F	W	2-0	Gascoigne, Mirandinha	28,583
23		2	(h)	Sheffield W	D	2-2	Goddard 2	25,503
24		23	(h)	Tottenham H	W	2-0	Gascoigne 2	24,616
25	Feb	6	(a)	Wimbledon	D	0-0		10,505
26		13	(h)	Norwich C	L	1-3	Gascoigne	21,068
27		27	(h)	Chelsea	W	3-1	Mirandinha 2, Gascoigne	17,858
28	Mar	1	(a)	Southampton	D	1-1	O'Neill	13,380
29		5	(a)	Everton	L	0-1		25,674
30		19	(a)	Arsenal	D	1-1	Goddard	25,889
31		26	(h)	Coventry C	D	2-2	O'Neill 2	19,050
32	Apr	2	(h)	Luton T	W	4-0	O'Neill 3, Goddard	20,565
33		4	(a)	Derby Co	L	1-2	O'Neill	18,591
34		9	(h)	QPR	D	1-1	O'Neill	18,403
35		12	(h)	Watford	W	3-0	O'Neill, Wharton, Tinnion	16,318
36		19	(a)	Watford	D	1-1	Anderson	12,075
37		23	(a)	Charlton A	L	0-2		7,482
38		30	(h)	Oxford U	W	3-1	Lormor, O'Neill, Goddard	16,617
39	May	2	(a)	Portsmouth	W	2-1	Scott, Lormor	12,468
40		7	(h)	West Ham U	W	2-1	O'Neill, Gascoigne	23,731

FINAL LEAGUE POSITION: 8th in Division One

Appearances

Sub Appearances

Goals

Kelly	McDonald	Bailey	McCreery	Jackson P.	Roeder	Jackson D.	Gascoigne	Goddard	Wharton	Hodges	Thomas A.	Scott	Thomas M.	Anderson	Mirandinha	Tinnion	Stephenson	Cornwell	O'Neill	Bogie	Craig	Lormor	No.
1	2	3	4	5	6	7*	8	9	10	11	12												1
1	2	3	4	5		7	8	9	10	11		6											2
	2	3	4	5	6	7	8	9†	10*	11		14	1	12									3
	2		4	5	6	7	8		3	11			1	10	9								4
	2		4	5	6		8	9	3	11			1	7	10								5
1	2		4†	5	6	12		9	8	11*				3	10	14	7						6
1	2		4	5	6	12		9	8	11*				3	10		7						7
1	7		4	5	6	12	8	9						2*	10	3		11					8
1	7†		4	5	6	12	8	9	14					2	10	3		11*					9
1	2		4*	5	6	7	8	9	12						10	3		11					10
1	2		4	5	6	7	8	9	14					12	10*	3		11†					11
1	7		4	5	6	10	8	9						2		3		11					12
1	7			5	6	11	8	9	4					2	10	3*		12					13
1	7*			5	6	10	8	9	4					2		3		11	12				14
1	7		4	5	6		8		3					2	9				10	11			15
1	7		4	5	6		8		3					2	10			11	9				16
1	7		4	5	6				3					2	10			11	9	8			17
1	7		4	5	6			9	3					2	10			11		8			18
1	7		4	5	6	12	8	9						2	10	3*		11					19
1	2		4		6	7†	8	9	3*			5		10				11	14	12			20
1	2		4		6	7*	8	9	3			5		10				11	12				21
1	7		4	5	6		8	9	3					2	10			11					22
1	7		4	5	6	11	8	9	3					2*	10†			12			14		23
1	7			5	6	4	8	9	3					2	10*			11			12		24
1	7			5	6	4	8	9	3					2	10			11					25
1	7			5	6	4*	8	9	3					2	10			12	11				26
1	2		4	5	6	12	8	9	3						10*	7		11					27
1	2		4	5	6		8	9	3						10	7		11					28
1	7		4*	5	6	12	8	9						2	10	3		11					29
1	2		4		6	10	8	9						5	3	12	7*	11					30
1	2		4		6	10	8	9						5	3		7*	11	12				31
1	2		4		6		8	9	11					5	3		7	10					32
1	2†		4		6		8	9	11					5	14	3	7*	12	10				33
1	7		4	5	6	11	8	9	3					2				10					34
1	2		4		6	7*	8	9	11					5	3		12	10					35
1	2		4		6		8	9	3			7*		5	10†			12	11		14		36
1	2		4		6		8	12	9	11				5	3*	7		10					37
1	2		4		6	7*	8	9	12					5	3			10				11	38
1	2	12	4		7		8	9						6	5	3		10*				11	39
1	2		4		7		8	9						6	5	3		10†	12			11	40
37	40	3	35	28	37	24	34	35	28	7	1	4	3	33	25	15	5	20	19	3	1	3	
	1						7	1		3			3		2	1	1	2	4	2	4	2	2	
	3		1	2	1	2	7	8	2			1		1	11	1		1	12			2	

51

1988-89

1	Aug	27	(a)	Everton	L	0-4	41,560
2	Sep	3	(h)	Tottenham H	D	2-2	Thorn, Jackson D.	32,977
3		10	(a)	Derby Co	L	0-2		16,014
4		17	(h)	Norwich C	L	0-2		22,801
5		24	(a)	Charlton A	D	2-2	Jackson D., Tinnion	6,088
6	Oct	1	(a)	Liverpool	W	2-1	Hendrie, Mirandinha (pen)	39,139
7		8	(h)	Coventry C	L	0-3		22,896
8		22	(a)	West Ham U	L	0-2		17,765
9		26	(h)	Middlesbrough	W	3-0	Pallister (og), Mirandinha 2	23,927
10		29	(h)	Nottingham F	L	0-1		24,765
11	Nov	5	(a)	QPR	L	0-3		11,013
12		12	(h)	Arsenal	L	0-1		24,033
13		19	(a)	Millwall	L	0-4		15,767
14		27	(h)	Manchester U	D	0-0		20,350
15	Dec	3	(a)	Luton T	D	0-0		8,338
16		10	(h)	Wimbledon	W	2-1	Hendrie 2	20,146
17		17	(h)	Southampton	D	3-3	Brock, O'Neill 2	19,986
18		26	(a)	Sheffield W	W	2-1	McDonald, O'Neill	25,573
19		31	(a)	Tottenham H	L	0-2		27,739
20	Jan	2	(h)	Derby Co	L	0-1		30,555
21		14	(a)	Aston Villa	L	1-3	Mirandinha (pen)	21,010
22		21	(h)	Charlton A	L	0-2		19,076
23	Feb	4	(h)	Liverpool	D	2-2	Mirandinha, Pingel	30,966
24		11	(a)	Coventry C	W	2-1	Hendrie, Mirandinha (pen)	16,577
25		26	(a)	Middlesbrough	D	1-1	O'Brien	24,385
26	Mar	11	(h)	QPR	L	1-2	Ranson	21,577
27		15	(a)	Nottingham F	D	1-1	Brock	20,800
28		22	(h)	Everton	W	2-0	Mirandinha, O'Brien	20,933
29		25	(a)	Norwich C	W	2-0	Mirandinha, O'Brien	22,440
30		27	(h)	Sheffield W	L	1-3	Mirandinha (pen)	31,040
31	Apr	1	(a)	Southampton	L	0-1		16,175
32		8	(h)	Aston Villa	L	1-2	O'Brien	20,329
33		15	(a)	Arsenal	L	0-1		38,023
34		22	(h)	Luton T	D	0-0		18,493
35		29	(a)	Wimbledon	L	0-4		5,206
36	May	3	(h)	West Ham U	L	1-2	Lormor	14,202
37		6	(h)	Millwall	D	1-1	Anderson	14,435
38		13	(a)	Manchester U	L	0-2		30,379

FINAL LEAGUE POSITION: 20th in Division One

Appearances

Sub Appearances

Goals

Beasant	Anderson	Tinnion	McCreery	Jackson P.	Thorn	Hendrie	Robertson	Mirandinha	Wharton	O'Neill	Jackson D.	Scott	Bogie	Craig	Stephenson	Cornwell	Payne	Robinson	O'Brien	McDonald	Roeder	Gourlay	Brock	Ranson	Sansom	Wright	Pingel	Brazil	Kelly	
1	2	3	4	5	6	7	8	9*	10	11	12																			1
1	2*		4		6	7	11		3	9	10	5	8	12																2
1	2		4		6	7	11		3	9	10	5	8																	3
1	2	3	4		6	7	11			9*	10	5	8		12															4
1	14		4		6	7	11†	9	3		10	5	12		8	2*														5
1	2		4		6	7	12	9	3	10*	8	5			11															6
1	2		4		6†	7	12	9	3	10*	8	5			11	14														7
1	2	3	4*		6†	8	12	9		11	10	5	14		7															8
1	2	3				8	12	9		10		4	5		7	6	11*													9
1	2	3				8	12	9		10		4	5		7	6	11*													10
1	2	3*	4		6	8	9			11	10	5			7		12													11
1	2	3	4		6	8	7*	9		10					5	11	12													12
1	2	3			6	8	12	11*		14					5†				7	9	10									13
1	2	3	4		6	7	10	12							5	11*			8	9										14
1	2	3	4		6	7	10*			9					5	11			8				12							15
1	2	3	4		6	7	10†	14		9*					5				8	12			11							16
1		3†	4	5		7		9*	10	12			14						2	8	6		11							17
1			4†			7	12	10		8*									14	9	6		11	2	3					18
1			4†			7	12	10		8*		5							14	9	6		11	2	3					19
1			4			7	9†	10*	12			5							14	8	6		11	2	3					20
			4			7			9	10		5					8*		6				11	2	3	1	12			21
	5		4†			7	12		10*	14		5							9		6		11	2	3	1	8			22
	5		4			7			9			2							10		6		11		3	1	8			23
	5		4			7			9*	12		2							10		6				3	1	8	11		24
			4			7			9*			5							10		6		11	2	3	1	8	12		25
			4			7*			12	14		5							10†		6		11	2	3	1	8	9		26
			4		6	7			12	14		5							10				11	2	3		8†	9*	1	27
			4		6	7	9†			14		5							10				11	2	3		8*	12	1	28
			4		6	7	9*			14		5							10				11	2	3		8†	12	1	29
			4		6	7	9			14		5							10				11	2†	3		8*	12	1	30
			4			7	9†		12			5							10		6		11	2	3		8*		1	31
			4			7	9*					5							10		6		11	2	3				1	32
			4		9	7			10			5								12	6				3		8*		1	33
			4		9	7	12	14	10*			5									6		11		3				1	34
			4		9				10			5								12	6		11	14	3		7*		1	35
	2†		4		9							5								12	6		11		3	1	10*			36
	2		4		6				8	10		5									6		11			1				37
	2		4		6				10*			5									6		11		3	1				38
20	21	12	36	1	26	34	7	22	14	17	13	29	3		7	8	6		17	6	18		21	13	20	9	13	3	9	
		1				5	6	4	10	2			3	1	1	1	1	1	3	4		1		1			1	4		
	1	1			1	4		9		3	2								4	1			2	1			1			

Match Number : -	31	32	33	34	35	36	37	38	Apps.	Sub.Apps	Goals
Sweeney	14	12	11†	8	8	8	3	8	5	2	
Kristensen			8	2	2†	2†	14		4	1	
Roche			14					14		2	
Lormor						7	7	7†	3		1
Howey								12		1	

Note : Lormor Scored in Match Nº 36

53

1989-90

1	Aug	19	(h)	Leeds U	W	5-2	Quinn 4 (1 pen), Gallacher	24,482
2		26	(a)	Leicester C	D	2-2	Quinn, Gallacher	13,384
3	Sep	2	(h)	Oldham A	W	2-1	Quinn 2 (1 pen)	20,804
4		9	(a)	Bournemouth	L	1-2	Quinn	9,882
5		13	(a)	Oxford U	L	1-2	Quinn	7,313
6		16	(h)	Portsmouth	W	1-0	Thorn	19,589
7		24	(a)	Sunderland	D	0-0		29,499
8		27	(h)	Watford	W	2-1	Gallacher, Quinn	17,040
9		30	(a)	Hull C	W	3-1	Anderson, Brazil, McGhee	9,629
10	Oct	7	(a)	Ipswich T	L	1-2	McGhee	13,679
11		14	(h)	Bradford C	W	1-0	McGhee	18,898
12		18	(h)	Blackburn R	W	2-1	McGhee, Quinn	20,702
13		21	(a)	Brighton & HA	W	3-0	Quinn 3	10,756
14		28	(h)	Port Vale	D	2-2	McGhee, Quinn	17,809
15	Nov	1	(a)	West Brom A	W	5-1	Robson (og), Brazil, Brock, McGhee, O'Brien	12,339
16		4	(h)	Middlesbrough	D	2-2	McGhee, O'Brien	23,349
17		11	(a)	West Ham U	D	0-0		25,892
18		18	(a)	Barnsley	D	1-1	Quinn	10,475
19		25	(h)	Sheffield U	W	2-0	Gallacher, Quinn	28,092
20	Dec	2	(a)	Leeds U	L	0-1		31,715
21		9	(h)	Oxford U	L	2-3	Stimson, Quinn (pen)	16,685
22		26	(a)	Stoke C	L	1-2	Scott	14,878
23		30	(a)	Swindon T	D	1-1	Quinn	11,657
24	Jan	1	(h)	Wolverhampton W	L	1-4	Brock	22,054
25		13	(h)	Leicester C	W	5-4	McGhee 2, Quinn 2, Gallacher	20,847
26		20	(a)	Oldham A	D	1-1	McGhee	11,194
27	Feb	4	(h)	Sunderland	D	1-1	McGhee	31,572
28		10	(a)	Portsmouth	D	1-1	Quinn	14,204
29		24	(a)	Sheffield U	D	1-1	Morris (og)	21,035
30		28	(h)	Bournemouth	W	3-0	Anderson, Quinn 2	15,119
31	Mar	3	(h)	Barnsley	W	4-1	Anderson, Scott, Aitken, McGhee (pen)	18,998
32		7	(h)	Hull C	W	2-0	McGhee 2 (1 pen)	20,499
33		10	(a)	Watford	D	0-0		12,069
34		17	(h)	Ipswich T	W	2-1	Quinn 2	19,521
35		21	(a)	Bradford C	L	2-3	McGhee (pen), Aizlewood (og)	10,264
36		24	(a)	Blackburn R	L	0-2		13,285
37		31	(h)	Brighton & HA	W	2-0	Gallacher, Quinn	18,746
38	Apr	3	(h)	Plymouth A	W	3-1	Quinn, McGhee 2 (1 pen)	16,558
39		7	(a)	Port Vale	W	2-1	Quinn, McGhee	10,290
40		11	(h)	West Brom A	W	2-1	Anderson, Quinn	19,460
41		14	(a)	Wolverhampton W	W	1-0	Scott	19,507
42		16	(h)	Stoke C	W	3-0	Kristensen 2, Quinn	26,190
43		21	(a)	Plymouth A	D	1-1	McGhee	11,702
44		25	(h)	Swindon T	D	0-0		26,568
45		28	(h)	West Ham U	W	2-1	Kristensen, Quinn	31,496
46	May	5	(a)	Middlesbrough	L	1-4	McGee (og)	18,484

FINAL LEAGUE POSITION: 3rd in Division Two

Appearances

Sub Appearances

Goals

54

Wright	Ranson	Sweeney	Dillon	Scott	Thorn	Gallacher	Brock	Quinn	McGhee	Fereday	Brazil	Stimson	Kristensen	Anderson	Kelly	Burridge	O'Brien	Bradshaw	Aitken	Robinson	Askew	
1	2	3*	4	5	6	7	8	9	10	11	12											1
1	2		4	5	6	7	8*	9	10	11		3	12									2
1	2†		4	5	6	7*	8	9	10	11	12	3	14									3
1	2	8*	4	5	6	7†		9	10	11		3	14	12								4
1	2	4*		5	6		8	9	10	11	7	3	12									5
	2			5	6	7	8	9	10	11		3	4*	12	1							6
			4	5	6	7*	8	9	10		12	3	11	2	1							7
			4	5	6	7	8	9	10	11		3		2	1							8
			4	5	6	7*	8	9†	10	11	12	3	14	2	1							9
			4	5	6†	7*	8	9	10	11	12	3	14	2		1						10
			4	5		7	8	9	10			3	6	2		1	11					11
			4	5		7*	8†	9	10	14	12	3	6	2		1	11					12
			4	5		7*	8	9	10	14	12	3	6	2†		1	11					13
	2		4	5			8	9	10	7		3	6			1	11					14
	2	14	4*	5			8	9	10	7	11†	3	6			1	12					15
	2†		4	5		14	8	9	10	7	11*	3	6			1	12					16
	2		4	5		14	8*	9	10	7†		3	6	12		1	11					17
	2*		4	5			8	9	10	7†	14	3	6	12		1	11					18
	2		4	5		7*	8	9	10	12		3	6			1	11					19
	2		4	5		7†	8	9	10	14		3*	6	12		1	11					20
	2	14	4*	5			8	9	10†	7		3	6	12		1	11					21
	2	3	4	5		7*	8	9	10	12†	14		6			1	11					22
		12		5			8	9	10	7*		3	6	2		1	11	4				23
				5		12	8	9	10	7		3	6	2		1	11	4*				24
		14	6†	5		12	8	9	10	7*		3		2		1	11		4			25
	7	3	6	5				9	10				8	2		1	11		4			26
	11†	8		5		7	14	9	10			3	6*	12		1		2	4			27
1	11	8		5		7		9	10			3	6*	12				2	4			28
1	6		8			7		9	10	11		3		5				2	4			29
1	6		8			7		9	10	11		3		5				2	4			30
1	6		8	2		12	7	9	10	11*		3		5					4			31
1	6	12	8	2		11	7	9	10			3*		5					4			32
1	6	3	8	2		11	7	9	10					5					4			33
1	6	3	8*			11†	7	9	10	12				5				2	4	14		34
1	6	3	8†			11*	7	9	10	12			14	5				2	4			35
1	6	3†	8	2			7	9	10	12				5				14*	4		11	36
	6	3	8	2		12	7	9	10					5		1			4		11	37
	6	3	8	2		12	7	9	10				14	5†		1			4		11	38
	6	3	8	2			7	9	10					5		1			4		11	39
	6	3	8	2			7	9	10	11*	12			5		1			4			40
	6		8	2			7	9	10			3	11	5		1			4			41
	6†		8*	2			7	9	10			3	11	5		1	12	14	4			42
			8	2			7	9	10			3	11	5		1		6	4			43
	6		8	2			7	9	10			3	11	5		1			4			44
	6		8*	2			7	9	10			3	11	5		1	12		4			45
	6		8	2†			7	9*	10			3	11	5		1	12	14	4			46
14	33	14	43	42	10	21	43	45	46	21	4	35	25	29	4	28	14	9	22		4	
	5						7	1		4	12	2	8	8		5	3			1		
			3	1	6	2		32	19		2	1	3	4			2			1		

1990-91

							Att
1	Aug	25	(h)	Plymouth A	W	2-0	Kristensen, Quinn	23,984
2	Sep	1	(a)	Blackburn R	W	1-0	O'Brien	11,329
3		8	(h)	Millwall	L	1-2	Quinn	23,922
4		15	(a)	Port Vale	W	1-0	Quinn	10,025
5		18	(a)	Sheffield W	D	2-2	McGhee 2	30,628
6		22	(h)	West Ham U	D	1-1	McGhee	25,462
7		29	(a)	Bristol C	L	0-1		15,858
8	Oct	3	(h)	Middlesbrough	D	0-0		17,023
9		6	(h)	Portsmouth	W	2-1	Quinn 2	17,682
10		13	(a)	Oxford U	D	0-0		6,820
11		20	(a)	Ipswich T	L	1-2	Quinn (pen)	15,567
12		24	(h)	Charlton A	L	1-3	Brock	14,016
13		27	(h)	West Brom A	D	1-1	O'Brien	14,774
14	Nov	3	(a)	Hull C	L	1-2	McGhee	8,375
15		10	(a)	Wolverhampton W	L	1-2	Clark	18,721
16		17	(h)	Barnsley	D	0-0		15,548
17		24	(h)	Watford	W	1-0	Quinn (pen)	13,774
18	Dec	1	(a)	Leicester C	L	4-5	Quinn 3, O'Brien	11,045
19		16	(a)	Plymouth A	W	1-0	Peacock	7,845
20		22	(a)	Bristol R	D	1-1	Gaynor	6,643
21		26	(h)	Swindon T	D	1-1	Quinn	17,003
22		29	(h)	Notts Co	L	0-2		17,557
23	Jan	1	(a)	Oldham A	D	1-1	Quinn	14,550
24		12	(h)	Blackburn R	W	1-0	Mitchell	16,382
25		16	(a)	Brighton & HA	L	2-4	Quinn, Brock	7,684
26		19	(a)	Millwall	W	1-0	Peacock	11,478
27	Feb	2	(h)	Port Vale	W	2-0	Peacock, Quinn	14,602
28		23	(h)	Wolverhampton W	D	0-0		18,612
29		27	(h)	Brighton & HA	D	0-0		12,692
30	Mar	2	(h)	Leicester C	W	2-1	McGhee, Sloan	13,575
31		9	(a)	Watford	W	2-1	Anderson, Quinn	10,018
32		12	(a)	Middlesbrough	L	0-3		18,250
33		16	(h)	Bristol C	D	0-0		13,578
34		23	(a)	Portsmouth	W	1-0	Brock	9,607
35		30	(a)	Swindon T	L	2-3	Peacock, Quinn	9,309
36	Apr	1	(h)	Bristol R	L	0-2		17,509
37		6	(a)	Notts Co	L	0-3		7,806
38		10	(h)	Oxford U	D	2-2	Hunt, Melville (og)	10,004
39		13	(h)	Oldham A	W	3-2	Peacock, Hunt, Brock	16,615
40		17	(h)	Sheffield W	W	1-0	Brock	18,330
41		20	(h)	Ipswich T	D	2-2	Stimson, Quinn	17,638
42		24	(a)	West Ham U	D	1-1	Peacock	24,195
43		27	(a)	Charlton A	L	0-1		7,234
44	May	4	(a)	West Brom A	D	1-1	Quinn	16,706
45		7	(a)	Barnsley	D	1-1	Peacock	9,534
46		11	(h)	Hull C	L	1-2	Clark	17,940

FINAL LEAGUE POSITION: 11th in Division Two

Appearances

Sub Appearances

Goals

56

Burridge	Scott	Sweeney	Aitken	Kristensen	Ranson	Dillon	Anderson	Quinn	Howey	O'Brien	McGhee	Brock	Fereday	Simpson	Bradshaw	Gourlay	Gallacher	Clark	Robinson	Sloan	Appleby	Askew	Roche	Watson S.	Stimson	Gaynor	Peacock	Mitchell	
1	2	3	4	5	6	7	8	9	10	11																			1
1	2	3	4	5	6	7	8	9	12	11	10*																		2
1	2	3	4	5	6	7*	8	9	12	11†	10	14																	3
1	2		4	5	6	7*	3	9		11	10	8†	12	14															4
1	2			5	6	7	3	9			10	8	11	12	4*														5
1	2		4	5	6	7	3*	9		14	10	8†	11	12															6
1	2		4	5	6			9			10		8*	3	7	11†	12	14											7
1	2	3	4	5*	6	7		9		11	10	8						12											8
1	2	3	4		6	7*	5	9		11	10	8						12											9
1	2		4		6		5	9		11	10	8	7*		3			12											10
1	2	3	4	10	14		5	9		11*		8	7		6†			12											11
1	2	14	4*	5	6		3†	9		11	10	8						12	7										12
1	2	3		5	6				12	11	10	9†						8		7*	4	14							13
1	2	3			6		5			11	10				9*			7		8		4	12						14
1	2				6		5	9		11*	10	3			4			7		8			12						15
1	2				6		3	9		11		8	12		4*			7		10					5				16
1	2		4	5	6			9		11		8								10						3	7		17
1	2		4	5	6			9		11		8						12		10						3	7*	6	18
1	5		4	6†	14		2	9		12		11						7*							3	10	8		19
1	5		4	6	12		2	9		7		11*													3	10	8		20
1	5		4	6	8	11	2	9		12		7								10*					3		8		21
1	5		4*	6	10	11	2	9		12		7†							14						3		8		22
1	5		4	6			2	9		12		7								10				11*	3		8		23
1			4	5	6	2	7	9		12														11	3		8*	10	24
1			4	6	5	10	2	9		7														11	3			8*	25
1			4	6	2	7*	5	9		11							12							10	3		8		26
1			4	6	2	7	5	9		11														10	3		8		27
1	5		4	6	2	7		9			12	11†												14	3		8		28
1	5		4	6	2	7		9			12	11												10	3		8*		29
1	5		4	6			2	9		12	10	11						7*							3		8		30
1	5		4	6			2†	9		7	10*	11													3		8		31
1	5		4	6				9		7		11†							12						3		8*		32
1	5		4	6				9	10†	12	14	11												2			8*		33
1	5		4	6		7		9	14	10*		11†												2	3		8		34
1	5		4		6	7		9				11												2	3		8		35
1	5		4	14	6	7†		9		12		11												2	3		8		36
1	5		4	6		7*		9	10†			11						12						2	3		8		37
1	5			6				9				11						7	12				4	2	3		8		38
1	5			6				9				11						7	12				4	2	3		8		39
	5			6				9	12	14		11						7†					4	2	3		8		40
	5			6				9	12	14		11						7					4†	2	3		8		41
	5			6				9	4			11						7						2			8		42
	5			6				9	12	4		11						7†					14	2	3		8		43
	5			6				9	12	4								7					11	2†			8		44
	5			6				9	12	4								7					14	2			8		45
	5			6				9		4	11							7						2			8		46
39	42	8	32	39	24	19	27	43	3	23	17	36	6	1	6	2	1	13		11	1	1	5	22	23	4	27	2	
	1		1	3					8	10	4	2	2		3		1	6	3	5		1	3	2					
					1		18			3	5	5						2					1		1	1	7	1	

1991-92

1	Aug	18	(a)	Charlton A	L	1-2	Carr	9,322
2		24	(h)	Watford	D	2-2	Hunt, Clark	22,440
3		27	(a)	Middlesbrough	L	0-3		16,970
4		31	(a)	Bristol R	W	2-1	O'Brien, Quinn	6,334
5	Sep	4	(h)	Plymouth A	D	2-2	Carr, Quinn	19,543
6		7	(a)	Tranmere R	L	2-3	O'Brien, Clark	11,465
7		14	(h)	Wolverhampton W	L	1-2	Madden (og)	20,195
8		17	(h)	Ipswich T	D	1-1	Quinn (pen)	16,336
9		21	(a)	Millwall	L	1-2	Neilson	9,156
10		28	(h)	Derby Co	D	2-2	Hunt, Quinn	17,581
11	Oct	5	(a)	Portsmouth	L	1-3	Quinn	10,175
12		12	(h)	Leicester C	W	2-0	Hunt, Clark	16,966
13		19	(h)	Oxford U	W	4-3	Hunt, Peacock	16,454
14		26	(a)	Bristol C	D	1-1	Clark	8,613
15	Nov	2	(a)	Swindon T	L	1-2	Peacock	10,731
16		6	(h)	Cambridge U	D	1-1	Hunt	13,077
17		9	(h)	Grimsby T	W	2-0	Hunt, Howey	16,959
18		17	(a)	Sunderland	D	1-1	O'Brien	29,224
19		20	(h)	Southend U	W	3-2	Peacock 2 (1 pen), Hunt	14,740
20		23	(h)	Blackburn R	D	0-0		23,639
21		30	(a)	Barnsley	L	0-3		9,648
22	Dec	7	(h)	Port Vale	D	2-2	Makel, Peacock (pen)	18,162
23		14	(a)	Brighton & HA	D	2-2	Peacock, Kelly	7,658
24		20	(a)	Plymouth A	L	0-2		5,048
25		26	(h)	Middlesbrough	L	0-1		26,563
26		28	(h)	Bristol R	W	2-1	Brock, Kelly	19,329
27	Jan	1	(a)	Southend U	L	0-4		9,458
28		11	(a)	Watford	D	2-2	Kelly, Hunt	9,811
29		18	(h)	Charlton A	L	3-4	Clark, Hunt, Brock	15,663
30	Feb	1	(a)	Oxford U	L	2-5	Scott, Peacock (pen)	5,872
31		8	(h)	Bristol C	W	3-0	Kelly 2, O'Brien	29,263
32		15	(a)	Blackburn R	L	1-3	Kelly	19,511
33		22	(h)	Barnsley	D	1-1	Kelly	27,670
34		29	(a)	Port Vale	W	1-0	Watson S.	10,321
35	Mar	7	(h)	Brighton & HA	L	0-1		24,597
36		10	(a)	Cambridge U	W	2-0	Peacock, Kelly	8,254
37		14	(h)	Swindon T	W	3-1	Kelly, Peacock, Quinn	23,138
38		21	(a)	Grimsby T	D	1-1	Sheedy	11,613
39		29	(h)	Sunderland	W	1-0	Kelly	30,306
40		31	(a)	Wolverhampton W	L	2-6	Quinn, Peacock	14,480
41	Apr	4	(h)	Tranmere R	L	2-3	Brock 2	21,125
42		11	(a)	Ipswich T	L	2-3	Peacock 2	20,673
43		18	(h)	Millwall	L	0-1		23,821
44		20	(a)	Derby Co	L	1-4	Peacock	21,363
45		25	(h)	Portsmouth	W	1-0	Kelly	25,989
46	May	2	(a)	Leicester C	W	2-1	Peacock, Walsh (og)	21,861

FINAL LEAGUE POSITION: 20th in Division Two

Appearances

Sub Appearances

Goals

58

	Smicek	Watson S	Elliott	O'Brien	Scott	Bradshaw	Clark	Peacock	Quinn	Carr	Brock	Roche	Robinson	Hunt	Neilson	Makel	Stimson	Howey	Walker	Appleby	Maguire	Wright	Thompson	Bodin	Kelly	Wilson	Ranson	Kilcline	Sheedy	
1	1	2†	3	4	5	6	7	8	9	10	11*	12	14																	1
2	1	2	3	4	5	6	7	8	9	10				11																2
3	1	12	3	4†	5	6	7	8	9	10		14		11*	2															3
4	1		3	4	5	6	7	8	9	10	11*				2	12														4
5	1		3	4	5	6	7	8†	9	10	11*			14	2	12														5
6	1	2	3	4	5	6	7	8	9	10	11*	12																		6
7	1		3	4	5	6	7	2	9	10	8			11																7
8	1			4	5	6	7	2	9	10*	8	12		11†			3	14												8
9	1			4	5	6	7	8	9		11			12	2		3		10*											9
10	1		3	4	5	6†	7	8	9		11	14		12	2				10*											10
11	1			4	5	6	7	8	9	12	11†			10*	2		3	14												11
12	1			4	5		7	8		11†	12	9*		10	2		3	14		6										12
13				4	5		7	8			11	12		10*	2		3	9		6		1								13
14				4	5		7	8*			11	12		10	2†	14	3	9		6		1								14
15				4	5		7	2	11		8			10*			3	9		6		1	12							15
16				4	5		7	2*	11		8			10		14	3†	9		6		1	12							16
17		12		4	5		7	2	11		8			10*			3	9		6		1	7							17
18		12		4	5		7	2*	11		8			14			3	9		6		1	10†							18
19		2		4	5		7		11	14	8	12		10*			3†	9		6		1								19
20		2	3	4	5		7		11*		8	12		10				9		6		1								20
21		2		4	5		7		11*	14	8	12		10			3	9		6†		1								21
22				4	5		7	8	11					10	2		3			6		1			9					22
23		12		4*	5		7	8	11					10	2		3			6		1			9					23
24		12		4	5		7†	8	11					10	2*	14	3			6		1			9					24
25		2		4*	5		7†	8	11			12		10		14	3			6		1			9					25
26		2		4	5		7	8	11			12		10*			3			6		1			9					26
27		2		4	5		7	8	11			12		10			3			6		1			9*					27
28		2		4	5		7	8	11			12		10			3*			6		1			9					28
29		2		4	5		7	8	11	14		12		10†			3			6		1			9*					29
30				4	5		7	8	11			12		10†	2	14	3*					1		6	9					30
31		7		4	5	6		8	11			12					3					1			9	10*	2			31
32		7		4	5		10	8	11			12					3					1		6	9	2*				32
33		2		4		6	7†	8	11	10*		12				14	3					1			9			5		33
34		7		4		6		8	11	10*		12			2		3					1			9			5		34
35		7*		4		6		8	11			12			2		3					1			9			5	10	35
36		2		4		6	7	8	11								3					1			9			5	10	36
37		2		4		6	7	8	11			12					3*					1			9			5	10	37
38		2				6	7	8	11			12					3					1			9			5	10	38
39		2		4		6	7	8	11								3					1			9			5	10	39
40		2		4		6	7	8	11								3					1			9		5*		10	40
41	1	2				6	7	8	11	12							3	5							9				10	41
42				4		6	7*	8	11			12					3	5				1			9		2†		10	42
43				4		6	7*	8	11			12					3					1			9			5	10	43
44		2		4		6	7*	8	11								3					1			9			5	10	44
45				4		6	7	8	11*			12		3								1			9		2	5	10	45
46				4		6	7	8	11*	12				3†								1			9		2	5	10	46
	13	23	9	40	44	17	25	46	18	12	31	18		21	16	5	23	13	2	16	3	33	12	6	25	2	5	12	13	
		5			2	4		4	3	4	8	3		6		4	1	8		2			2			1				
	1			4	1		5	16	7	2	4			9	1	1		1							11				1	

1992-93

1	Aug	15	(h)	Southend U	W 3-2	Bracewell, Prior (og), Clark	28,545
2		22	(a)	Derby Co	W 2-1	Peacock, Clark	17,522
3		29	(h)	West Ham U	W 2-0	Peacock, Kelly	29,855
4	Sep	2	(h)	Luton T	W 2-0	Clark, Kelly	27,054
5		5	(a)	Bristol R	W 2-1	Sheedy, O'Brien	7,487
6		12	(h)	Portsmouth	W 3-1	Quinn 2, Kelly	29,885
7		19	(h)	Bristol C	W 5-0	O'Brien, Peacock 2 (2 pens), Carr, Brock	29,465
8		26	(a)	Peterborough U	W 1-0	Sheedy	14,487
9	Oct	4	(a)	Brentford	W 2-1	Kelly, Peacock	10,131
10		13	(h)	Tranmere R	W 1-0	Kelly	30,137
11		18	(a)	Sunderland	W 2-1	Owers (og), O'Brien	28,098
12		24	(h)	Grimsby T	L 0-1		30,088
13		31	(a)	Leicester C	L 1-2	O'Brien	19,687
14	Nov	4	(a)	Birmingham C	W 3-2	Peacock, Scott, Matthewson (og)	14,376
15		8	(h)	Swindon T	D 0-0		28,091
16		14	(a)	Charlton A	W 3-1	Peacock 2, Howey	12,945
17		21	(h)	Watford	W 2-0	Peacock, Lee	28,871
18		28	(h)	Cambridge U	W 4-1	Kelly 3, Peacock	27,991
19	Dec	5	(a)	Notts Co	W 2-0	Sheedy, Peacock	14,840
20		13	(a)	Barnsley	L 0-1		13,263
21		20	(h)	Millwall	D 1-1	Kelly (pen)	26,089
22		26	(h)	Wolverhampton W	W 2-1	Kelly 2	30,137
23		28	(a)	Oxford U	L 2-4	O'Brien, Clark	9,293
24	Jan	9	(a)	Bristol C	W 2-1	Kelly, Scott	15,446
25		16	(h)	Peterborough U	W 3-0	Lee 2, Kelly	29,155
26		20	(a)	Southend U	D 1-1	Peacock	8,246
27		27	(a)	Luton T	D 0-0		10,237
28		31	(h)	Derby Co	D 1-1	O'Brien	27,285
29	Feb	9	(a)	Portsmouth	L 0-2		21,028
30		21	(a)	West Ham U	D 0-0		24,159
31		24	(h)	Bristol R	D 0-0		29,372
32		28	(a)	Tranmere R	W 3-0	Lee 2, Kelly	13,082
33	Mar	6	(h)	Brentford	W 5-1	Kelly, Bracewell, Clark 2, Lee	30,006
34		10	(h)	Charlton A	D 2-2	Lee, Kelly	29,582
35		13	(a)	Swindon T	L 1-2	Kelly	17,574
36		20	(h)	Notts Co	W 4-0	Lee, Kelly 2, Cole	30,029
37		23	(a)	Watford	L 0-1		11,634
38		28	(h)	Birmingham C	D 2-2	Cole, Lee	27,087
39	Apr	3	(a)	Cambridge U	W 3-0	Howey, Kelly, Cole	7,925
40		7	(h)	Barnsley	W 6-0	Cole 3, Clark, Beresford, Sellars	29,460
41		10	(a)	Wolverhampton W	L 0-1		17,244
42		17	(a)	Millwall	W 2-1	Clark, Cole	14,262
43		25	(h)	Sunderland	W 1-0	Sellars	30,364
44	May	4	(a)	Grimsby T	W 2-0	Kelly, Cole	14,402
45		6	(h)	Oxford U	W 2-1	Clark, Cole	29,438
46		9	(h)	Leicester C	W 7-1	Cole 3, Lee, Kelly 3	30,129

FINAL LEAGUE POSITION: 1st in Division One

Appearances

Sub Appearances

Goals

60

Wright	Venison	Beresford	Bracewell	Kilcline	Howey	Watson	Peacock	Kelly	Clark	Sheedy	Scott	Carr	Ranson	O'Brien	Quinn	Thompson	Brock	Lee	Neilson	Smicek	Stimson	Robinson	Sellars	Cole	No.
1	2	3	4	5	6	7	8	9	10	11															1
1	2	3		5	4		8	9	10	11	6	7													2
1	2				6		8	9	10	11	5	7	3	4											3
1	2				6		8	9	10	11	5	7	3	4											4
1	2		12†	13	6		8*	9	10	11	5	7	3	4											5
1	2	3			6			9*	10	11	5	7		4	8	12									6
1	2	3			6		8	9	10	11*	5	7†		4	12		13								7
1	2	3			6			9	10	11	5			4	8*		12	7							8
1	2	3			6		8	9	10	11	5			4				7							9
1	2	3			6		8	9	10		5			4	11			7							10
1	2	3			6		8	9	10		5			4			11	7							11
1	2*	3	13	12	6		8		10		5			4	9		11†	7							12
1		3		12	6		8	9	10	11	5			4				7*	2						13
1*	2	3		13	6		8	9	10	11†	5	7		4			12								14
	2	3			6		8	9	10	11	5	7		4						1					15
	2	3	11		6		8	9	10		5			4				7		1					16
	2	3	11	12	6*		8	9	10		5	13		4				7†		1					17
	2	3			6		8	9	10		5			4			11	7		1					18
	2	3			6		8	9	10	11	5			4				7		1					19
	2	3			6		8	9	10	11	5			4				7		1					20
	2	3*	8	12	6			9	10	11†	5	13		4				7		1					21
	2				6		8	9	10	11	5			4				7	3	1					22
	2	3	12		6		8*	9	10	11	5			4				7		1					23
	2	3	12		6		8	9	10	11*	5			4				7		1					24
	2	3	12		6		8	9	10	11*	5			4				7		1					25
	2	3			6		8	9	10		5			4			11	7		1					26
	2	3	11		6		8	9	10		5			4				7		1					27
	2	3	12	13	6		8	9†	10	11*	5			4				7		1					28
	2	3	11*	5			8	9	10	12	6			4				7		1					29
	2	3			6		8	9	10	11	5			4				7		1					30
	2	3			6	12	8	9	10	11*	5			4				7		1					31
	2	3	13	12†	6		8	9	10	11	5*			4				7		1					32
	2	3	8		6*			9	10		5			4				7	12	1	11				33
		3	8		6			9	10		5			4				7		1	12	2	11*		34
	2	3	8		6			9	10		5			4*				7		1			11	12	35
	2	3	4		6		13	9	10†		5*							7		1		12	11	8	36
	2	3	4		6			9	10		5							7		1		12	11*	8	37
	2	3	4		6			9	10		5							7		1			11	8	38
	2	3	4*		6			9	10		5							7		1		12	11	8	39
	2	3	4*	13	6†			9	10		5							7		1		12	11	8	40
	2	3	4	13	6		9†		10		5							7		1		12	11*	8	41
	2	3	4	6				9	10		5							7		1		12	11	8*	42
	2	3	4		6			9	10		5							7		1			11	8	43
	2	3	4		6			9	10		5							7		1			11	8	44
	2	3	4†		6		13	9	10		5							7*		1		12	11	8	45
	2	3*		13	6†		12	9	10		5							7		1		4	11	8	46
14	44	42	19	7	41	1	29	45	46	23	45	8	3	33	4	1	4	36	2	32	1	2	13	11	
		6	12		1		3			1		2			1	1	3		1		1		7	1	
		1	2	2			12	24	9	3	2	1		6	2		1	10					2	12	

1993-94

1	Aug	14	(h)	Tottenham H	L	0-1		34,565
2		18	(a)	Coventry C	L	1-2	Atherton (og)	15,763
3		21	(a)	Manchester U	D	1-1	Cole	41,829
4		25	(h)	Everton	W	1-0	Allen	34,490
5		29	(h)	Blackburn R	D	1-1	Cole	33,987
6		31	(a)	Ipswich T	D	1-1	Cole	19,126
7	Sep	13	(h)	Sheffield W	W	4-2	Cole 2, Mathie, Allen	33,519
8		18	(a)	Swindon T	D	2-2	Clark, Allen (pen)	15,393
9		25	(h)	West Ham U	W	2-0	Cole 2	34,179
10	Oct	2	(a)	Aston Villa	W	2-0	Allen (pen), Cole	37,366
11		16	(h)	QPR	L	1-2	Allen	33,801
12		24	(a)	Southampton	L	1-2	Cole	13,804
13		30	(h)	Wimbledon	W	4-0	Beardsley 3 (1 pen), Cole	33,371
14	Nov	8	(a)	Oldham Ath	W	3-1	Cole 2, Beardsley	13,821
15		21	(h)	Liverpool	W	3-0	Cole 3	36,246
16		24	(h)	Sheffield U	W	4-0	Ward (og), Beardsley 2 (1 pen), Cole	35,029
17		27	(a)	Arsenal	L	1-2	Beardsley	36,091
18	Dec	4	(a)	Tottenham H	W	2-1	Beardsley 2	30,780
19		11	(h)	Manchester U	D	1-1	Cole	36,332
20		18	(a)	Everton	W	2-0	Cole, Beardsley	25,362
21		22	(h)	Leeds U	D	1-1	Cole	36,388
22		28	(a)	Chelsea	L	0-1		23,133
23	Jan	1	(h)	Manchester C	W	2-0	Cole 2	35,585
24		4	(a)	Norwich C	W	2-1	Beadsley, Cole	19,564
25		16	(a)	QPR	W	2-1	Clark, Beardsley	15,774
26		22	(h)	Southampton	L	1-2	Cole	32,067
27	Feb	12	(a)	Wimbledon	L	2-4	Beardsley 2 (2 pens)	13,358
28		19	(a)	Blackburn R	L	0-1		20,798
29		23	(h)	Coventry C	W	4-0	Cole 3, Mathie	32,210
30	Mar	5	(a)	Sheffield W	W	1-0	Cole	33,153
31		12	(h)	Swindon T	W	7-1	Beardsley 2 (1 pen), Lee 2, Watson 2, Fox	32,219
32		19	(a)	West Ham U	W	4-2	Lee 2, Cole, Mathie	23,132
33		23	(h)	Ipswich T	W	2-0	Sellars, Cole	32,234
34		29	(h)	Norwich C	W	3-0	Cole, Lee, Beardsley	32,228
35	Apr	1	(a)	Leeds U	D	1-1	Cole	40,005
36		4	(h)	Chelsea	D	0-0		32,218
37		9	(a)	Manchester C	L	1-2	Sellars	33,774
38		16	(a)	Liverpool	W	2-0	Lee, Cole	44,601
39		23	(h)	Oldham Ath	W	3-2	Fox, Beardsley, Lee	32,214
40		27	(h)	Aston Villa	W	5-1	Bracewell, Beardsley 2 (1 pen), Cole, Sellars	32,217
41		30	(a)	Sheffield U	L	0-2		29,013
42	May	7	(h)	Arsenal	W	2-0	Cole, Beardsley (pen)	32,216

FINAL LEAGUE POSITION : 3rd in Premiership

Appearances

Sub. Appearances

Goals

Smicek	Venison	Beresford	Bracewell	Scott	Howey	Lee	Allen	Cole	Clark	Papavasiliou	O'Brien	Watson	Wright	Neilson	Mathie	Beardsley	Hooper	Sellars	Elliott	Jeffrey	Robinson	Kilcline	Fox	Appleby	Holland	Peacock	
1	2	3	4	5	6	7	8†	9	10	11*	12	14															1
1	2	3	4	5		7		9	10	11*	6	8	12														2
1	2	3	4	5		7		9	10	11	6	8															3
1	2	3	4	5			8	9	10	11	6	7															4
1	2	3	4	5		7		9	10	11	6	8															5
1	2	3	4	5		7	8	9	10*	11†	12	6		14													6
	2	3	4	5		7	8	9	10	11*		6	1		12												7
	2	3	4	5		7	11	9	10			6	1			8											8
	2	3	4	5		7	11	9	10			6				8	1										9
	2	3	4	5		7	11	9	10			6				8	1										10
	2	3	4	5		7	11	9	10			6				8	1										11
	2	3	4	5		7	11†	9	10*			6			12	8	1	14									12
	2	3	4	5		7		9	10			6				8	1	11									13
	2		4	5		7		9	10			6				8	1	11	3								14
	2		4	5		7		9	10			6				8	1	11	3								15
	2		4*	5		7		9	10			6			12	8	1	11	3								16
	2		4	5	14	7		9	10†			6			12	8	1	11	3*								17
	2		4	5		7		9	10			6				8	1		3	11							18
	2		4	5		7		9	10			6				8	1	11	3								19
	2	3*	4	5		7		9	10			6				8	1	11	12								20
	2	3	4	5		7		9	10*			6			12	8	1	11									21
	2	3	4	5		7		9	10*			6†			12	8	1	11			14						22
		3	4†		6	7		9	10			14			12	8	1	11			2*	5					23
		3		5	6	7		9	10							8	1	11	4		2						24
	2	3	4		6	7		9	10							8	1	11			5						25
	2	3	4		6	7		9	10							8	1	11			5						26
	2	3		5				9*	10			6			12	8	1	11	4				7				27
1	2	3		5				9	10			6				8		11	4				7				28
1						7†		9	10		2		5	12		8		11*	3	14			6	4			29
1		3	4*			7		9				6		5		8		11	12		2		10				30
1		3	4			7		9				6				8		11	5		2		10				31
1		3	4			7		9				6†	14	12		8		11	5		2		10*				32
1		3	4			7		9				6*	14	12		8		11	5†		2		10				33
1		3	4†			7		9				6		12		8		11			2		10*		14	5	34
1	12	3	4			7*		9				6				8		11			2		10			5	35
1	6	3†	4			7		9					14	12		8		11			2		10*			5	36
1		3				7		9				6		12		8		11	10*		2		4			5	37
1	2†	3	4			7		9				6		12		8*		11	14				10			5	38
1	2	3	4			7		9				6				8		11					10			5	39
1	2	3	4†			7		9*			14	6		12		8		11					10			5	40
1	2	3	4			7		9				6				8		11					10			5	41
1	2	3				7		9			4*	6		12		8		11					10			5	42
21	36	34	32	18	13	41	9	40	29	7	4	29	2	10		35	19	29	13	2	12	1	14	1	2	9	
	1		1							2	3	1	4	16			1	2		4				1			
		1			7	5	34	2			2			3	21			3			2						

63

1994-95

1	Aug	21	(a)	Leicester C	W	3-1	Cole, Beardsley, Elliott	20,048
2		24	(h)	Coventry C	W	4-0	Lee 2, Watson, Cole	34,163
3		27	(h)	Southampton	W	5-1	Watson 2, Cole 2, Lee	34,182
4		31	(a)	West Ham U	W	3-1	Potts (og), Lee, Mathie	17,375
5	Sep	10	(h)	Chelsea	W	4-2	Cole 2, Fox, Lee	34,435
6		18	(a)	Arsenal	W	3-2	Keown (og), Beardsley (pen), Fox	36,819
7		24	(h)	Liverpool	D	1-1	Lee	34,435
8	Oct	1	(a)	Aston Villa	W	2-0	Lee, Cole	29,960
9		9	(h)	Blackburn R	D	1-1	Flowers (og)	34,344
10		15	(a)	Crystal Palace	W	1-0	Beardsley	17,739
11		22	(h)	Sheffield W	W	2-1	Watson, Cole	34,369
12		29	(a)	Manchester U	L	0-2		43,795
13	Nov	5	(h)	QPR	W	2-1	Kitson, Beardsley	34,278
14		7	(a)	Nottingham F	D	0-0		22,102
15		19	(a)	Wimbledon	L	2-3	Beardsley, Kitson	14,203
16		26	(h)	Ipswich T	D	1-1	Cole	34,459
17	Dec	3	(a)	Tottenham H	L	2-4	Fox 2	28,002
18		10	(h)	Leicester C	W	3-1	Albert 2, Howey	34,400
19		17	(a)	Coventry C	D	0-0		17,237
20		26	(a)	Leeds U	D	0-0		39,337
21		31	(a)	Norwich C	L	1-2	Fox (pen)	21,172
22	Jan	2	(h)	Manchester C	D	0-0		34,437
23		15	(h)	Manchester U	D	1-1	Kitson	34,471
24		21	(a)	Sheffield W	D	0-0		31,215
25		25	(h)	Wimbledon	W	2-1	Fox, Kitson	34,374
26	Feb	1	(h)	Everton	W	2-0	Fox, Beardsley (pen)	34,465
27		4	(a)	QPR	L	0-3		16,576
28		11	(h)	Nottingham F	W	2-1	Fox, Lee	34,471
29		25	(h)	Aston Villa	W	3-1	Venison, Beardsley 2	34,637
30		28	(a)	Ipswich T	W	2-0	Fox, Kitson	18,639
31	Mar	4	(a)	Liverpool	L	0-2		39,300
32		8	(h)	West Ham U	W	2-0	Clark, Kitson	34,595
33		19	(h)	Arsenal	W	1-0	Beardsley	35,611
34		22	(a)	Southampton	L	1-3	Kitson	14,666
35	Apr	1	(a)	Chelsea	D	1-1	Hottiger	22,987
36		8	(h)	Norwich C	W	3-0	Beardsley 2 (1 pen), Kitson	35,518
37		14	(a)	Everton	L	0-2		34,628
38		17	(h)	Leeds U	L	1-2	Elliott	35,626
39		29	(a)	Manchester C	D	0-0		27,389
40	May	3	(h)	Tottenham H	D	3-3	Gillespie, Peacock, Beardsley	35,603
41		8	(a)	Blackburn R	L	0-1		30,545
42		14	(h)	Crystal Palace	W	3-2	Fox, Lee, Gillespie	35,626

FINAL LEAGUE POSITION : 6th in F.A. Carling Premiership

Appearances

Sub. Appearances

Goals

Smicek	Hottiger	Beresford	Venison	Peacock	Albert	Lee	Beardsley	Cole	Fox	Sellars	Elliott	Mathie	Hooper	Watson	Howey	Kitson	Neilson	Clark	Bracewell	Gillespie	Allen	
1	2	3	4	5	6	7	8†	9	10	11*	12	14°	15									1
1	2	3	4	5	6	7		9	10	11*	12	14		8†								2
1	2	3	4	5	6	7		9	10†	11*	12	14		8								3
1	2	3	4	5	6	7*		9		11	12	10		8								4
	2	3	4	5	6	7		9	10	11			1	8								5
1	2	3		5	6	7	8	9	10	11					4							6
1	2	3	4†	5	6	7	8	9	10	11*				12	14							7
1	2	3		5	6	7	8*	9	10	11					4	12						8
1	2	3		5		7*	8	9	10	11				6	4	12						9
1		3			6		8	9	10	11				5	4	7	2					10
1	2	3		5	6		8	9	10	11				4		7*		12				11
1	2*	3		5	6	9	8		10†	11		12		7	4			14				12
1	2	3		5	6	9	8		10					7	4	11						13
1	2	3		5	6	9	8		10					7		11		4				14
1	2	3	7	5†	6	9	8		10					12	4	11*		14				15
1	2	3	4		6†	7*	8	9	10		12			11			5	14				16
1	2	3	4				8	9	10			7°		6			5	11				17
1	2	11	4	5	3		8	9	10					7	6							18
1	2	3	4	5			8*	9	10					7	6	11		12				19
1		3	2		6	7		9	10					4	5	11			8			20
1		3	2	5		7		9	10					6*	4	11		12	8			21
1		3	2	5		7	8	9	10						6	11		4				22
1	2	3	4	5		7			10	11					6	9		8				23
1	2	3	4	5		7*	8		10						6	9		11	12			24
1	2		4	5			8		10		3				6	9			7	11		25
	2		4			7	8		10		3*	9	1				5	12	6	11		26
	2					7	8				3	12	1	4		9*	5	10	6	11		27
1	2	3	4	5		7	8		10						6	9			12	11*		28
1	2	3	4	5		7	8		10						6	9				11		29
1	2	3	4	5		7	8		10						6	9				11		30
1	2	3	4	5		7	8*		10†					12	6	9			14	11		31
1	2	3	4	5		7			10					12	6†	9*		8	14	11		32
1	2		4	5		7*	8		10		3					9		12	6	11		33
1	2		4	5		7	8		10		3				6	9				11		34
1	2		4	5		7*	8		10		3			14	6	9†		12	11			35
1	2		4	5		7	8		10		3				6	9				11		36
	2*		4	5		7	8		10†		3		1		6	9		12	11	14		37
1	2					7	8		10		3*			5	6	9	12		4	11		38
1	2	3		5			8		10					4	6			11	7	9		39
1	2	3		5		7	8		10°			15		11	6			4*	9	12		40
1	2	3		5		7	8		10					4	6			11		9		41
1	2	3		5		7	8		10					4	6			11		9		42
38	38	33	28	35	17	35	34	18	40	12	10	3	4	22	29	24	5	9	13	15		
											4	6	2	5	1	2	1	10	3	2	1	
	1		1	1	2	9	12	9	10		2	1		4	1	8		1		2		

SEASON 1977-78 (cont.)

Barton	McGhee	Parkinson	Scott	Guy	
6*	10				23
	9				24
	9				25
					26
	10*				27
	10	12			28
	10	12			29
4	10		7		30
4	10		7		31
4	10				32
4	10				33
4	10		12		34
4	9		11		35
4	9		11		36
4	9		11*		37
4	9		11		38
4			11		39
4	12				40
4	9				41
4	9*			7	42
14	17		7	1	Appearances
		1	2	1	Sub Appearances
	3				Goals

SEASON 1990-91 (cont.)

Moran	Hunt	Neilsen	Elliott	Srnicek	Makel	Watson J.	
10*							28
							29
							30
	12	14					31
	10	2	14				32
	7	3					33
	12						34
	10						35
10*							36
	14						37
10*							38
10*							39
10*				1			40
10*				1			41
10			3	1			42
10*			3	1			43
10*			3	1	14		44
10*			3†	1	11		45
10*			3†	1	12	14	46
1	13	2	5	7	1	-	Appearances
-	3	1	1	-	2	1	Sub Appearances
	2						Goals

SEASON 1991-92 (cont.)

McDonough	Kristensen	Garland	
4*			38
			39
12			40
4*			41
	14		42
	2†	14	43
			44
			45
		14	46
2	1	-	Appearances
1	1	2	Sub Appearances
			Goals

1970-71 SEASON

FIRST DIVISION

Arsenal	42	29	7	6	71	29	65
Leeds United	42	27	10	5	72	30	64
Tottenham Hotspur	42	19	14	9	54	33	52
Wolves	42	22	8	12	64	54	52
Liverpool	42	17	17	8	42	24	51
Chelsea	42	18	15	9	52	42	51
Southampton	42	17	12	13	56	44	46
Manchester United	42	16	11	15	65	66	43
Derby County	42	16	10	16	56	54	42
Coventry City	42	16	10	16	37	38	42
Manchester City	42	12	17	13	47	42	41
Newcastle United	**42**	**14**	**13**	**15**	**44**	**46**	**41**
Stoke City	42	12	13	17	44	48	37
Everton	42	12	13	17	54	60	37
Huddersfield Town	42	11	14	17	40	49	36
Nottingham Forest	42	14	8	20	42	61	36
West Brom. Albion	42	10	15	17	58	75	35
Crystal Palace	42	12	11	19	39	57	35
Ipswich Town	42	12	10	20	42	48	34
West Ham United	42	10	14	18	47	60	34
Burnley	42	7	13	22	29	63	27
Blackpool	42	4	15	23	34	66	23

1971-72 SEASON

FIRST DIVISION

Derby County	42	24	10	8	69	33	58
Leeds United	42	24	9	9	73	31	57
Liverpool	42	24	9	9	64	30	57
Manchester City	42	23	11	8	77	45	57
Arsenal	42	22	8	12	58	40	52
Tottenham Hotspur	42	19	13	10	63	42	51
Chelsea	42	18	12	12	58	49	48
Manchester United	42	19	10	13	69	61	48
Wolves	42	18	11	13	65	57	47
Sheffield United	42	17	12	13	61	60	46
Newcastle United	**42**	**15**	**11**	**16**	**49**	**52**	**41**
Leicester City	42	13	13	16	41	46	39
Ipswich Town	42	11	16	15	39	53	38
West Ham United	42	12	12	18	47	51	36
Everton	42	9	18	15	37	48	36
West Brom. Albion	42	12	11	19	42	54	35
Stoke City	42	10	15	17	39	56	35
Coventry City	42	9	15	18	44	67	33
Southampton	42	12	7	23	52	80	31
Crystal Palace	42	8	13	21	39	65	29
Nottingham Forest	42	8	9	25	47	81	25
Huddersfield Town	42	6	13	23	27	59	25

1972-73 SEASON

FIRST DIVISION

Liverpool	42	25	10	6	72	42	60
Arsenal	42	23	11	8	57	43	57
Leeds United	42	21	11	10	71	45	53
Ipswich Town	42	17	14	11	55	45	48
Wolves	42	18	11	13	66	54	47
West Ham United	42	17	12	13	67	53	46
Derby County	42	19	8	15	56	54	46
Tottenham Hotspur	42	16	13	13	58	48	45
Newcastle United	**42**	**16**	**13**	**13**	**60**	**51**	**45**
Birmingham City	42	15	12	15	53	54	42
Manchester City	42	15	11	16	57	60	41
Chelsea	42	13	14	15	49	51	40
Southampton	42	11	18	13	47	52	40
Sheffield United	42	15	10	17	51	59	40
Stoke City	42	14	10	18	61	56	38
Leicester City	42	10	17	15	40	46	37
Everton	42	13	11	18	41	49	37
Manchester United	42	12	13	17	44	60	37
Coventry City	42	13	9	20	40	55	35
Norwich City	42	11	10	21	36	63	32
Crystal Palace	42	9	12	21	41	58	30
West Brom. Albion	42	9	10	23	38	62	28

1973-74 SEASON

FIRST DIVISION

Leeds United	42	24	14	4	66	31	62
Liverpool	42	22	13	7	52	31	57
Derby County	42	17	14	11	52	42	48
Ipswich Town	42	18	11	13	67	58	47
Stoke City	42	15	16	11	54	42	46
Burnley	42	16	14	12	56	53	46
Everton	42	16	12	14	50	48	44
Q.P.R.	42	13	17	12	56	52	43
Leicester City	42	13	16	13	51	41	42
Arsenal	42	14	14	14	49	51	42
Tottenham Hotspur	42	14	14	14	45	50	42
Wolves	42	13	15	14	49	49	41
Sheffield United	42	14	12	16	44	49	40
Manchester City	42	14	12	16	39	46	40
Newcastle United	**42**	**13**	**12**	**17**	**49**	**48**	**38**
Coventry City	42	14	10	18	43	54	38
Chelsea	42	12	13	17	56	60	37
West Ham United	42	11	15	16	55	60	37
Birmingham City	42	12	13	17	52	64	37
Southampton *	42	11	14	17	47	68	36
Manchester United *	42	10	12	20	38	48	32
Norwich City *	42	7	15	20	37	62	29

* Three clubs relegated

1974-75 SEASON

FIRST DIVISION

Derby County	42	21	11	10	67	49	53
Liverpool	42	20	11	11	60	39	51
Ipswich Town	42	23	5	14	66	44	51
Everton	42	16	18	8	56	42	50
Stoke City	42	17	15	10	64	48	49
Sheffield United	42	18	13	11	58	51	49
Middlesbrough	42	18	12	12	54	40	48
Manchester City	42	18	10	14	54	54	46
Leeds United	42	16	13	13	57	49	45
Burnley	42	17	11	14	68	67	45
Q.P.R.	42	16	10	16	54	54	42
Wolves	42	14	11	17	57	54	39
West Ham United	42	13	13	16	58	59	39
Coventry City	42	12	15	15	51	62	39
Newcastle United	**42**	**15**	**9**	**18**	**59**	**72**	**39**
Arsenal	42	13	11	18	47	49	37
Birmingham City	42	14	9	19	53	61	37
Leicester City	42	12	12	18	46	60	36
Tottenham Hotspur	42	13	8	21	52	63	34
Luton Town	42	11	11	20	47	65	33
Chelsea	42	9	15	18	42	72	33
Carlisle United	42	12	5	25	43	59	29

1975-76 SEASON

FIRST DIVISION

Liverpool	42	23	14	5	66	31	60
Q.P.R.	42	24	11	7	67	33	59
Manchester United	42	23	10	10	68	42	56
Derby County	42	21	11	10	75	58	53
Leeds United	42	21	9	12	65	46	51
Ipswich Town	42	16	14	12	54	48	46
Leicester City	42	13	19	10	48	51	45
Manchester City	42	16	12	15	64	46	43
Tottenham Hotspur	42	14	15	13	63	63	43
Norwich City	42	16	10	16	58	58	42
Everton	42	15	12	15	60	66	42
Stoke City	42	15	11	16	48	50	41
Middlesbrough	42	15	10	17	46	45	40
Coventry City	42	13	14	15	47	57	40
Newcastle United	**42**	**15**	**9**	**18**	**71**	**62**	**39**
Aston Villa	42	11	17	14	51	59	39
Arsenal	42	13	10	19	47	53	36
West Ham United	42	13	10	19	48	71	36
Birmingham City	42	13	7	22	57	75	33
Wolves	42	10	10	22	51	68	30
Burnley	42	9	10	23	43	66	28
Sheffield United	42	6	10	26	33	82	22

1977-78 SEASON

FIRST DIVISION

Nottingham Forest	42	25	14	3	69	24	64
Liverpool	42	24	9	9	65	34	57
Everton	42	22	11	9	76	45	55
Manchester City	42	20	12	10	74	51	52
Arsenal	42	21	10	11	60	37	52
West Brom. Albion	42	18	14	10	62	53	50
Coventry City	42	18	12	12	75	62	48
Aston Villa	42	18	10	14	57	42	46
Leeds United	42	18	10	14	63	53	46
Manchester United	42	16	10	16	67	63	42
Birmingham City	42	16	9	17	55	60	41
Derby County	42	14	13	15	54	59	41
Norwich City	42	11	18	13	52	66	40
Middlesbrough	42	12	15	15	42	54	39
Wolves	42	12	12	18	51	64	36
Chelsea	42	11	14	17	46	69	36
Bristol City	42	11	13	18	49	53	35
Ipswich Town	42	11	13	18	47	61	35
Q.P.R.	42	9	15	18	47	64	33
West Ham United	42	12	8	22	52	69	32
Newcastle United	**42**	**6**	**10**	**26**	**42**	**78**	**22**
Leicester City	42	5	12	25	26	70	22

1976-77 SEASON

FIRST DIVISION

Liverpool	42	23	11	8	62	33	57
Manchester City	42	21	14	7	60	34	56
Ipswich Town	42	22	8	12	66	39	52
Aston Villa	42	22	7	13	76	50	51
Newcastle United	**42**	**18**	**13**	**11**	**64**	**49**	**49**
Manchester United	42	18	11	13	71	62	47
West Brom. Albion	42	16	13	13	62	56	45
Arsenal	42	16	11	15	64	59	43
Everton	42	14	14	14	62	64	42
Leeds United	42	15	12	15	48	51	42
Leicester City	42	12	18	12	47	60	42
Middlesbrough	42	14	13	15	40	45	41
Birmingham City	42	13	12	17	63	61	38
Q.P.R.	42	13	12	17	47	52	38
Derby County	42	9	19	14	50	55	37
Norwich City	42	14	9	19	47	64	37
West Ham United	42	11	14	17	46	65	36
Bristol City	42	11	13	18	38	48	35
Coventry City	42	10	15	17	48	59	35
Sunderland	42	11	12	19	46	54	34
Stoke City	42	10	14	18	28	51	34
Tottenham Hotspur	42	12	9	21	48	72	33

1978-79 SEASON

SECOND DIVISION

Crystal Palace	42	19	19	4	51	24	57
Brighton & Hove Alb.	42	23	10	9	72	39	56
Stoke City	42	20	16	6	58	31	56
Sunderland	42	22	11	9	70	44	55
West Ham United	42	18	14	10	70	39	50
Notts County	42	14	16	12	48	60	44
Preston North End	42	12	18	12	59	57	42
Newcastle United	**42**	**17**	**8**	**17**	**51**	**55**	**42**
Cardiff City	42	16	10	16	56	70	42
Fulham	42	13	15	14	50	47	41
Orient	42	15	10	17	51	51	40
Cambridge United	42	12	16	14	44	52	40
Burnley	42	14	12	16	51	62	40
Oldham Athletic	42	13	13	16	52	61	39
Wrexham	42	12	14	16	45	42	38
Bristol Rovers	42	14	10	18	48	60	38
Leicester City	42	10	17	15	43	52	37
Luton Town	42	13	10	19	60	57	36
Charlton Athletic	42	11	13	18	60	69	35
Sheffield United	42	11	12	19	52	69	34
Millwall	42	11	10	21	42	61	32
Blackburn Rovers	42	10	10	22	41	72	30

1979-80 SEASON

SECOND DIVISION

Leicester City	42	21	13	8	58	38	55
Sunderland	42	21	12	9	69	42	54
Birmingham City	42	21	11	10	58	38	53
Chelsea	42	23	7	12	66	52	53
Q.P.R.	42	18	13	11	75	53	49
Luton Town	42	16	17	9	66	45	49
West Ham United	42	20	7	15	54	43	47
Cambridge United	42	14	16	12	61	53	44
Newcastle United	**42**	**15**	**14**	**13**	**53**	**49**	**44**
Preston North End	42	12	19	11	56	52	43
Oldham Athletic	42	16	11	15	49	53	43
Swansea City	42	17	9	16	48	53	43
Shrewsbury Town	42	18	5	19	60	53	41
Orient	42	12	17	13	48	54	41
Cardiff City	42	16	8	18	41	48	40
Wrexham	42	16	6	20	40	49	38
Notts County	42	11	15	16	51	52	37
Watford	42	12	13	17	39	46	37
Bristol Rovers	42	11	13	18	50	64	35
Fulham	42	11	7	24	42	74	29
Burnley	42	6	15	21	39	73	27
Charlton Athletic	42	6	10	26	39	78	22

1980-81 SEASON

SECOND DIVISION

	P	W	D	L	F	A	Pts
West Ham United	42	28	10	4	79	29	66
Notts County	42	18	17	7	49	38	53
Swansea City	42	18	14	10	64	44	50
Blackburn Rovers	42	16	18	8	42	29	50
Luton Town	42	18	12	12	61	46	48
Derby County	42	15	15	12	57	52	45
Grimsby Town	42	15	15	12	44	42	45
QPR	42	15	13	14	56	46	43
Watford	42	16	11	15	50	45	43
Sheffield Wednesday	42	17	8	17	53	51	42
Newcastle United	**42**	**14**	**14**	**14**	**30**	**45**	**42**
Chelsea	42	14	12	16	46	41	40
Cambridge United	42	17	6	17	53	65	40
Shrewsbury Town	42	11	17	14	46	47	39
Oldham Athletic	42	12	15	15	39	48	39
Wrexham	42	12	14	16	43	45	38
Orient	42	13	12	17	52	56	38
Bolton Wanderers	42	14	10	18	61	66	38
Cardiff City	42	12	12	18	44	60	36
Preston North End	42	11	14	17	41	62	36
Bristol City	42	7	16	19	29	51	30
Bristol Rovers	42	5	13	24	34	65	23

1981-82 SEASON

SECOND DIVISION

	P	W	D	L	F	A	Pts
Luton Town	42	25	13	4	86	46	88
Watford	42	23	11	8	76	42	80
Norwich City	42	22	5	15	64	50	71
Sheffield Wednesday	42	20	10	12	55	51	70
QPR	42	21	6	15	65	43	69
Barnsley	42	19	10	13	59	41	67
Rotherham United	42	20	7	15	66	54	67
Leicester City	42	18	12	12	56	48	66
Newcastle United	**42**	**18**	**8**	**16**	**52**	**50**	**62**
Blackburn Rovers	42	16	11	15	47	43	59
Oldham Athletic	42	15	14	13	50	51	59
Chelsea	42	15	12	15	60	60	57
Charlton Athletic	42	13	12	17	50	65	51
Cambridge United	42	13	9	20	48	53	48
Crystal Palace	42	13	9	20	34	45	48
Derby County	42	12	12	18	53	68	48
Grimsby Town	42	11	13	18	53	65	46
Shrewsbury Town	42	11	13	18	37	57	46
Bolton Wanderers	42	13	7	22	39	61	46
Cardiff City	42	12	8	22	45	61	44
Wrexham	42	11	11	20	40	56	44
Orient	42	10	9	23	39	61	39

1982-83 SEASON

SECOND DIVISION

	P	W	D	L	F	A	Pts
Q.P.R.	42	26	7	9	77	36	85
Wolves	42	20	15	7	68	44	75
Leicester City	42	20	10	12	72	44	70
Fulham *	42	20	9	13	64	47	69
Newcastle United	**42**	**18**	**13**	**11**	**75**	**53**	**67**
Sheffield Wednesday	42	16	15	11	60	47	63
Oldham Athletic	42	14	19	9	64	47	61
Leeds United	42	13	21	8	51	46	60
Shrewsbury Town	42	15	14	13	48	48	59
Barnsley	42	14	15	13	57	55	57
Blackburn Rovers	42	15	12	15	58	58	57
Cambridge United	42	13	12	17	42	60	51
Derby County *	42	10	19	13	49	58	49
Carlisle United	42	12	12	18	68	70	48
Crystal Palace	42	12	12	18	43	52	48
Middlesbrough	42	11	15	16	46	67	48
Charlton Athletic	42	13	9	20	63	86	48
Chelsea	42	11	14	17	51	61	47
Grimsby Town	42	12	11	19	45	70	47
Rotherham United	42	10	15	17	45	68	45
Burnley	42	12	8	22	56	66	44
Bolton Wanderers	42	11	11	20	42	61	44

* Game between Derby and Fulham abandoned after 88 minutes but result allowed to stand at 1-0.

1983-84 SEASON

SECOND DIVISION

	P	W	D	L	F	A	Pts
Chelsea	42	25	13	4	90	40	88
Sheffield Wednesday	42	26	10	6	72	34	88
Newcastle United	**42**	**24**	**8**	**10**	**85**	**53**	**80**
Manchester City	42	20	10	12	66	48	70
Grimsby Town	42	19	13	10	60	47	70
Blackburn Rovers	42	17	16	9	57	46	67
Carlisle United	42	16	16	10	48	41	64
Shrewsbury Town	42	17	10	15	49	53	61
Brighton & Hove Alb.	42	17	9	16	69	60	60
Leeds United	42	16	12	14	55	56	60
Fulham	42	15	12	15	60	53	57
Huddersfield Town	42	14	15	13	56	49	57
Charlton Athletic	42	16	9	17	53	64	57
Barnsley	42	15	7	20	57	53	52
Cardiff City	42	15	6	21	53	66	51
Portsmouth	42	14	7	21	73	64	49
Middlesbrough	42	12	13	17	41	47	49
Crystal Palace	42	12	11	19	42	52	47
Oldham Athletic	42	13	8	21	47	73	47
Derby County	42	11	9	22	36	72	42
Swansea City	42	7	8	27	36	85	29
Cambridge United	42	4	12	26	28	77	24

1984-85 SEASON

FIRST DIVISION

	P	W	D	L	F	A	Pts
Everton	42	28	6	8	88	43	90
Liverpool	42	22	11	9	78	35	77
Tottenham Hotspur	42	23	8	11	78	51	77
Manchester United	42	22	10	10	77	47	76
Southampton	42	19	11	12	56	47	68
Chelsea	42	18	12	12	63	48	66
Arsenal	42	19	9	14	61	49	66
Sheffield Wednesday	42	17	14	11	58	45	65
Nottingham Forest	42	19	7	16	56	48	64
Aston Villa	42	15	11	16	60	60	56
Watford	42	14	13	15	81	71	55
West Brom	42	16	7	19	58	62	55
Luton Town	42	15	9	18	57	61	54
Newcastle United	**42**	**13**	**13**	**16**	**55**	**70**	**52**
Leicester City	42	15	6	21	65	73	51
West Ham United	42	13	12	17	51	68	51
Ipswich Town	42	13	11	18	46	57	50
Coventry City	42	15	5	22	47	64	50
QPR	42	13	11	18	53	72	50
Norwich City	42	13	10	19	46	64	49
Sunderland	42	10	10	22	40	62	40
Stoke City	42	3	8	31	24	91	17

1985-86 SEASON

FIRST DIVISION

Liverpool	42	26	10	6	89	37	88
Everton	42	26	8	8	87	41	86
West Ham United	42	26	6	10	74	40	84
Manchester United	42	22	10	10	70	36	76
Sheffield Wednesday	42	21	10	11	63	54	73
Chelsea	42	20	11	11	57	56	71
Arsenal	42	20	9	13	49	47	69
Nottingham Forest	42	19	11	12	69	53	68
Luton Town	42	18	12	12	61	44	66
Tottenham Hotspur	42	19	8	15	74	52	65
Newcastle United	**42**	**17**	**12**	**13**	**67**	**72**	**63**
Watford	42	16	11	15	69	62	59
QPR	42	15	7	20	53	64	52
Southampton	42	12	10	20	51	62	46
Manchester City	42	11	12	19	43	57	45
Aston Villa	42	10	14	18	51	67	44
Coventry City	42	11	10	21	48	71	43
Oxford United	42	10	12	20	62	80	42
Leicester City	42	10	12	20	54	76	42
Ipswich Town	42	11	8	23	32	55	41
Birmingham City	42	8	5	29	30	73	29
West Brom	42	4	12	26	35	89	24

1986-87 SEASON

FIRST DIVISION

Everton	42	26	8	8	76	31	86
Liverpool	42	23	8	11	72	42	77
Tottenham Hotspur	42	21	8	13	68	43	71
Arsenal	42	20	10	12	58	35	70
Norwich City	42	17	17	8	53	51	68
Wimbledon	42	19	9	14	57	50	66
Luton Town	42	18	12	12	47	45	66
Nottingham Forest	42	18	11	13	64	51	65
Watford	42	18	9	15	67	54	63
Coventry City	42	17	12	13	50	45	63
Manchester United	42	14	14	14	52	45	56
Southampton	42	14	10	18	69	68	52
Sheffield Wednesday	42	13	13	16	58	59	52
Chelsea	42	13	13	16	53	64	52
West Ham United	42	14	10	18	52	67	52
QPR	42	13	11	18	48	64	50
Newcastle United	**42**	**12**	**11**	**19**	**47**	**65**	**47**
Oxford United	42	11	13	18	44	69	46
Charlton Athletic	42	11	11	20	45	55	44
Leicester City	42	11	9	22	54	76	42
Manchester City	42	8	15	19	36	57	39
Aston Villa	42	8	12	22	45	79	36

1987-88 SEASON

FIRST DIVISION

Liverpool	40	26	12	2	87	24	90
Manchester United	40	23	12	5	71	38	81
Nottingham Forest	40	20	13	7	67	39	73
Everton	40	19	13	8	53	27	70
QPR	40	19	10	11	48	38	67
Arsenal	40	18	12	10	58	39	66
Wimbledon	40	14	15	11	58	47	57
Newcastle United	**40**	**14**	**14**	**12**	**55**	**53**	**56**
Luton Town	40	14	11	15	57	58	53
Coventry City	40	13	14	13	46	53	53
Sheffield Wednesday	40	15	8	17	52	66	53
Southampton	40	12	14	14	49	53	50
Tottenham Hotspur	40	12	11	17	38	48	47
Norwich City	40	12	9	19	40	52	45
Derby County	40	10	13	17	35	45	43
West Ham United	40	9	15	16	40	52	42
Charlton Athletic	40	9	15	16	38	52	42
Chelsea	40	9	15	16	50	68	42
Portsmouth	40	7	14	19	36	66	35
Watford	40	7	11	22	27	51	32
Oxford United	40	6	13	21	44	80	31

1988-89 SEASON

FIRST DIVISION

Arsenal	38	22	10	6	73	36	76
Liverpool	38	22	10	6	65	28	76
Nottingham Forest	38	17	13	8	64	43	64
Norwich City	38	17	11	10	48	45	62
Derby County	38	17	7	14	40	38	58
Tottenham Hotspur	38	15	12	11	60	46	57
Coventry City	38	14	13	11	47	42	55
Everton	38	14	12	12	50	45	54
QPR	38	14	11	13	43	37	53
Millwall	38	14	11	13	47	52	53
Manchester United	38	13	12	13	45	35	51
Wimbledon	38	14	9	15	50	46	51
Southampton	38	10	15	13	52	66	45
Charlton Athletic	38	10	12	16	44	58	42
Sheffield Wednesday	38	10	12	16	34	51	42
Luton Town	38	10	11	17	42	52	41
Aston Villa	38	9	13	16	45	56	40
Middlesbrough	38	9	12	17	44	61	39
West Ham United	38	10	8	20	37	62	38
Newcastle United	**38**	**7**	**10**	**21**	**32**	**63**	**31**

1989-90 SEASON

SECOND DIVISION

Leeds United	46	24	13	9	79	52	85
Sheffield United	46	24	13	9	78	58	85
Newcastle United	**46**	**22**	**14**	**10**	**80**	**55**	**80**
Swindon Town	46	20	14	12	79	59	74
Blackburn Rovers	46	19	17	10	74	59	74
Sunderland	46	20	14	12	70	64	74
West Ham United	46	20	12	14	80	57	72
Oldham Athletic	46	19	14	13	70	57	71
Ipswich Town	46	19	12	15	67	66	69
Wolves	46	18	13	15	67	60	67
Port Vale	46	15	16	15	62	57	61
Portsmouth	46	15	16	15	62	65	61
Leicester City	46	15	14	17	67	79	59
Hull City	46	14	16	16	58	65	58
Watford	46	14	15	17	58	60	57
Plymouth Argyle	46	14	13	19	58	63	55
Oxford United	46	15	9	22	57	66	54
Brighton & Hove Alb.	46	15	9	22	56	72	54
Barnsley	46	13	15	18	49	71	54
West Brom	46	12	15	19	67	71	51
Middlesbrough	46	13	11	22	52	63	50
Bournemouth	46	12	12	22	57	76	48
Bradford City	46	9	14	23	44	68	41
Stoke City	46	6	19	21	35	63	37

1990-91 SEASON

SECOND DIVISION

Team	P	W	D	L	F	A	Pts
Oldham Athletic	46	25	13	8	83	53	88
West Ham United	46	24	15	7	60	34	87
Sheffield Wednesday	46	22	16	8	80	51	82
Notts County	46	23	11	12	76	55	80
Millwall	46	20	13	13	70	51	73
Brighton & Hove Alb.	46	21	7	18	63	69	70
Middlesbrough	46	20	9	17	66	47	69
Barnsley	46	19	12	15	63	48	69
Bristol City	46	20	7	19	68	71	67
Oxford United	46	14	19	13	69	66	61
Newcastle United	**46**	**14**	**17**	**15**	**49**	**56**	**59**
Wolves	46	13	19	14	63	63	58
Bristol Rovers	46	15	13	18	56	59	58
Ipswich Town	46	13	18	15	60	68	57
Port Vale	46	15	12	19	56	64	57
Charlton Athletic	46	13	17	16	57	61	56
Portsmouth	46	14	11	21	58	70	53
Plymouth Argyle	46	12	17	17	54	68	53
Blackburn Rovers	46	14	10	22	51	66	52
Watford	46	12	15	19	45	59	51
Swindon Town	46	12	14	20	65	73	50
Leicester City	46	14	8	24	60	83	50
West Brom	46	10	18	18	52	61	48
Hull City	46	10	15	21	57	85	45

1991-92 SEASON

SECOND DIVISION

Team	P	W	D	L	F	A	Pts
Ipswich Town	46	24	12	10	70	50	84
Middlesbrough	46	23	11	12	58	41	80
Derby County	46	23	9	14	69	51	78
Leicester City	46	23	8	15	62	55	77
Cambridge United	46	19	17	10	65	47	74
Blackburn Rvrs	46	21	11	14	70	53	74
Charlton Athletic	46	20	11	15	54	48	71
Swindon Town	46	18	15	13	69	55	69
Portsmouth	46	19	12	15	65	51	69
Watford	46	18	11	17	51	48	65
Wolves	46	18	10	18	61	54	64
Southend United	46	17	11	18	63	63	62
Bristol Rovers	46	16	14	16	60	63	62
Tranmere Rovers	46	14	19	13	56	56	61
Millwall	46	17	10	19	64	71	61
Barnsley	46	16	11	19	46	57	59
Bristol City	46	13	15	18	55	71	54
Sunderland	46	14	11	21	61	65	53
Grimsby Town	46	14	11	21	47	62	53
Newcastle United	**46**	**13**	**13**	**20**	**66**	**84**	**52**
Oxford United	46	13	11	22	66	73	50
Plymouth Argyle	46	13	9	24	42	64	48
Brighton & Hove Alb.	46	12	11	23	56	77	47
Port Vale	46	10	15	21	42	59	45

1992-93 SEASON

FIRST DIVISION

Team	P	W	D	L	F	A	Pts
Newcastle United	**46**	**29**	**9**	**8**	**92**	**38**	**96**
West Ham United	46	26	10	10	81	41	88
Portsmouth	46	26	10	10	80	46	88
Tranmere Rovers	46	23	10	13	72	56	79
Swindon Town	46	21	13	12	74	59	76
Leicester City	46	22	10	14	71	64	76
Millwall	46	18	16	12	65	53	70
Derby County	46	19	9	18	68	57	66
Grimsby Town	46	19	7	20	58	57	64
Peterborough United	46	16	14	16	55	63	62
Wolves	46	16	13	17	57	56	61
Charlton Athletic	46	16	13	17	49	46	61
Barnsley	46	17	9	20	56	60	60
Oxford United	46	14	14	18	53	56	56
Bristol City	46	14	14	18	49	67	56
Watford	46	14	13	19	57	71	55
Notts County	46	12	16	18	55	70	52
Southend United	46	13	13	20	54	64	52
Birmingham City	46	13	12	21	50	72	51
Luton Town	46	10	21	15	48	62	51
Sunderland	46	13	11	22	50	64	50
Brentford	46	13	10	23	52	71	49
Cambridge United	46	11	16	19	48	69	49
Bristol Rovers	46	10	11	25	55	87	41

1993-94 SEASON

F.A. PREMIERSHIP

Team	P	W	D	L	F	A	Pts
Manchester United	42	27	11	4	80	38	92
Blackburn Rovers	42	25	9	8	63	36	84
Newcastle United	**42**	**23**	**8**	**11**	**82**	**41**	**77**
Arsenal	42	18	17	7	53	28	71
Leeds United	42	18	16	8	65	39	70
Wimbledon	42	18	11	13	56	53	65
Sheffield Wednesday	42	16	16	10	76	54	64
Liverpool	42	17	9	16	59	55	60
QPR	42	16	12	14	62	64	60
Aston Villa	42	15	12	15	46	50	57
Coventry City	42	14	14	14	43	45	56
Norwich City	42	12	17	13	65	61	53
West Ham United	42	13	13	16	47	58	52
Chelsea	42	13	12	17	49	53	51
Tottenham Hotspur	42	11	12	19	54	59	45
Manchester City	42	9	18	15	38	49	45
Everton	42	12	8	22	42	63	44
Southampton	42	12	7	23	49	66	43
Ipswich Town	42	9	16	17	35	58	43
Sheffield United	42	8	18	16	42	60	42
Oldham Athletic	42	9	13	20	42	68	40
Swindon Town	42	5	15	22	47	100	30

1993-94 SEASON

F.A. PREMIERSHIP

Team	P	W	D	L	F	A	Pts
Blackburn Rovers	42	27	8	7	80	39	89
Manchester United	42	26	10	6	77	28	88
Nottingham Forest	42	22	11	9	72	43	77
Liverpool	42	21	11	10	65	37	74
Leeds United	42	20	13	9	59	38	63
Newcastle United	**42**	**20**	**12**	**10**	**67**	**47**	**72**
Tottenham Hotspur	42	16	14	12	66	58	62
QPR	42	17	9	16	61	59	60
Wimbledon	42	15	11	16	48	65	56
Southampton	42	12	18	12	61	63	54
Chelsea	42	13	15	14	50	55	54
Arsenal	42	13	12	17	52	49	51
Sheffield Wednesday	42	13	12	17	49	57	51
West Ham United	42	13	11	18	44	48	50
Everton	42	11	17	14	44	51	50
Coventry City	42	12	14	16	44	62	50
Manchester City	42	12	13	17	53	64	49
Aston Villa	42	11	15	16	51	56	48
Crystal Palace	42	11	12	19	34	49	45
Norwich City	42	10	13	19	37	54	43
Leicester City	42	6	11	25	45	80	29
Ipswich Town	42	7	6	29	36	93	27

FOOTBALL UNDER THE SKIN

An 80-page book giving a historical glimpse of Soccer on Tyne & Wear 1879-1988. Packed with illustrations.

Priced £4.95 post free

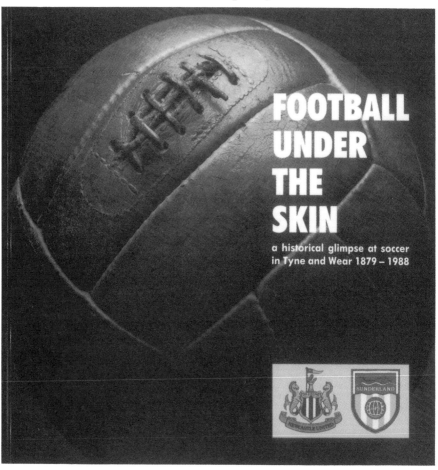

available from : -

THE SOCCER BOOKSHELF (SBP)
72 ST. PETERS AVENUE
CLEETHORPES
SOUTH HUMBERSIDE
DN35 8HU